Becoming
GREAT

Loving A Culture In Conflict

Greg Wallace

VΙƆ⅃Ε

For Worldwide Distribution.

Vide Press
6200 Second Street
Washington D.C. 20011
www.VidePress.com

ISBN: 978-1-954618-31-2 (Print)
ISBN: 978-1-954618-32-9 (ebook)

Published in the United States of America

Cover Design by Miblart.com

Table of Contents

Prologue

"What would Jesus do?" was a popular question back in the 1990s. "WWJD" appeared on bracelets, necklaces, bumper stickers, and t-shirts. The first essay I ever wrote for publication turned this question on its head.

In the essay, I asked, what would we do if Jesus returned? Would we welcome Him? Or would we, as the people in Luke 4 did, throw Him out of the city?

I mention this essay because it is one of the first places where I articulated the importance of service motivated by Christlike love. Service motivated by Christlike love is a primary theme of my speaking, writing, and motivations. It is also the glue that holds the collection of essays in *Becoming Great* together.

I wrote the essays[1] at different times and for different contexts. There are blogs, white papers, chapters in books, and documentation of personal encounters with the Lord. I have revised a few of the essays for this book. All have been edited (thank you, Lord!)

Each one supports the central premise of the book. If we are to make America great, it won't be through the

---

1   Essays are defined as "an analytic or interpretative literary composition usually dealing with its subject from a limited or personal point of view". *Merriam-Webster.com Dictionary*, s.v. "essay," accessed August 21, 2021, https://www.merriam-webster.com/dictionary/essay.

exercise of authority. We will make America great by answering God's call to serve others.

What if the words Jesus spoke to His disciples in Matthew 20:25-26 were spoken to the leaders in America? "Kings and those with great authority in this world rule oppressively over their subjects, like tyrants. But this is not your calling, America. You will lead by a completely different model. The greatest one among the nations will live as the one who is called to serve others."

An America that becomes "the greatest one" among nations because it answered God's call to serve others can truly make disciples of all nations. It starts with each one of us answering that call.

So, let's begin with my first essay. Not because it is so well-written. But because it sets the context for what is to follow. I wrote the original version of the essay more than ten years ago. I updated it five years ago. That is the version I included here.

# # #

When Jesus appeared in the synagogue at Jerusalem and spoke the words captured in Luke 4:18 and 19, the synagogue was a well-established part of the community. Its leaders were the unquestioned authorities on all things spiritual.

But as we all know, Jesus didn't think very highly of the synagogue's leaders, and they didn't think highly of Him. In fact, in Luke's account, they chased Jesus out of the synagogue.

If Jesus came back to earth, we'd all like to think that we would avoid the same mistake and welcome Jesus with open arms. But would we?

Before answering this question, let's take a moment to think about Jesus' approach with the "church leaders" of His day. Jesus did not wait for a pastor's invitation to address the congregation; He spoke directly to the people. He did not create programs to meet needs; He commissioned people to meet needs; He did not ask people to give to His ministry; He asked people to give. He was not interested in growing membership; He was interested in growing the body of Christ.

It's fair to say that Jesus did not focus on the church leaders of His day; He focused on people. It's also fair to say that most church leaders did not respond well to this approach.

So how would we respond to Jesus' approach?

Would we challenge the status quo as Jesus did ("You have heard that it was said ... but I tell you...") or would we challenge the things that are challenging the status quo as the Pharisees did ("By what authority are you doing these things?")

One way to challenge the status quo is to challenge the traditional view of Ephesians 4:11-12: *And he has appointed some with grace to be apostles, and some with grace to be prophets, and some with grace to be evangelists, and some with grace to be pastors, and some with grace to be teachers. And their calling is to nurture and prepare all the holy believers to do their own works of ministry, and as they do this they will enlarge and build up the body of Christ.*

The "traditional" mindset is that church leaders decide on acts of service, and they recruit people to work in a church ministry to perform those acts of service. The people support the church leaders. In other words, service is pastor- or apostle-led.

In a transformation culture, people, motivated by Christlike love, decide on and perform acts of service in their sphere of influence. Church leaders support *them*. Jesus gave us the five-fold ministry gifts to equip the people so that the people could serve. Thus, service is not pastor-led or apostle-led but "saint-led." Acts of service may be performed by individuals or in small groups of people, or by members of a ministry, but service is always love-led.

Introduction

Americans are known for their rugged individualism. Our ruggedness contributes to a daring spirit. It is a spirit that fueled the expansion of a thirteen-colony confederation hugging one coast into a fifty-state republic that stretches from the Atlantic into the Pacific. It invented the airplane, landed the first humans on the moon, and still produces billionaires in bunches.

Our individualism contributes to a self-confidence (some might say arrogance) that views America as the center of the world. To our way of thinking, our president is the leader of the free world. The Midwest is the breadbasket of the world. Silicon Valley is the high-tech center of the world. And our military is the world's policeman.

If Americans are rugged individualists, so, too, are American Christians. Many of us identify with Peter, the most daring and the most self-confident (some might say, arrogant) of Jesus' disciples.

Peter had enough self-confidence to *tell* Jesus to command him to walk on water. He had enough daring to step out onto the water when Jesus called him. American Christians have enough self-confidence to proclaim the United States as a Christian nation and enough daring to make Christian nations of other countries.

But just as Peter's self-confidence and daring didn't prevent him from noticing stormy weather, American Christians can't help but notice the storm clouds gathering on America's cultural horizon.

As noted by a *Newsweek* article published in January 2021[2], many in the American Church believe that religious liberty is under attack, our values are under attack, and our existence as the Church is under attack.

When Peter began to pay more attention to the storm than he did to Jesus, he started to sink. With our eyes focused on "attacks" rather than Jesus, the American Church is also beginning to sink. We are making fewer disciples, not more.

According to surveys conducted by the Pew Research Center in 2018 and 2019, the number of American adults who describe themselves as Christian is down twelve percentage points over the past decade.[3] Meanwhile, the religiously unaffiliated share of the population increased from 17 percent to 26 percent.[4]

To prevent sinking from turning into drowning (to protect our liberty, uphold our values, and ensure our continued existence), some Christian leaders have expanded their focus beyond the American Church to American culture.

---

2   See, Paul Bond, "Christians, Including Pastor Receiving Death Threats, in Crosshairs After Capitol Riot," *Newsweek*, January 19, 2021, accessed https://www.newsweek.com/christians-including-pastor-receiving-death-threats-crosshairs-after-capitol-riot-1562253

3   See, "In U.S., Decline of Christianity Continues at Rapid Pace: An update on America's changing religious landscape," *Pew Research Center*, October 17, 2019, accessed https://www.pewforum.org/2019/10/17/in-u-s-decline-of-christianity-continues-at-rapid-pace/

4   See, "In U.S., Decline of Christianity Continues at Rapid Pace"

They believe a culture war is being waged in America and the American Church is a "combatant." Said one commentator:[5] "Two worldviews are locked in mortal combat right now in our politics, our popular culture, and our courts and legal system."[6]

However, some Christian leaders seem to have lost confidence in spiritual weapons to win the culture war. Even as we "pray harder, worship longer, fast more frequently, intensify spiritual warfare, and live more holy lives," noted one highly respected leader, American society is "moving further and further away from Kingdom principles, not closer."[7]

Thus, we have adopted an approach to establishing Kingdom principles similar to the world's approach. "We need believers in positions of power … in order to see our communities impacted by the presence of the King and His Kingdom," said one Christian leader.[8] "We need more disciples in the right place, the high places," said another.[9]

---

5   You may notice that the number of times that Christian leaders are mentioned by name in the text is relatively rare. This is intentional. There are two reasons for this decision. Unfortunately, certain names have become lightning rods in our discussions. The mere mention of the name is enough to discredit the comment regardless of the merits of the comment. However, proper attribution is provided in footnotes or endnotes. And to the extent I am critical of a comment, I want to focus my criticism on the comment not the commentator.

6   See, Alan Sears, "The Election and Religious Freedom: The essential freedoms we have cherished so long are no longer a given for any of us." *Decisions*. November 2, 2016, accessed https://decisionmagazine.com/53293-2/

7   C. Peter Wagner, *This Changes Everything: How God Can Transform Your Mind And Change Your Life* (Chosen Books. Bloomington, MN 2013), 191-192

8   Lance Wallnau, Bill Johnson, *Invading Babylon: The 7 Mountain Mandate,* (Destiny Image. Shippensburg, PA 2013), 13

9   See, Wallnau, Johnson, *Invading Babylon,* 64

Though Jesus calls on us to serve rather than exercise "great authority,"[10] we, like the world, seek to exert influence through the exercise of power and authority.

"To be on top (of the high places) means to amass the most power and/or the most wealth," said one Christian leader. He believes the chief producer of influence "is not spirituality but success. The most successful people are the most influential."[11]

But even if we "amass the most power" and become influential through our success at electing candidates who protect religious liberties, appointing judges who overturn rulings we do not like, and passing legislation that reflects our values, the American Church will continue to sink, i.e., it will continue to lose influence with the culture we are trying to win for Christ.

Moreover, there are signs that society is infiltrating the Church, not vice versa. Rather than society reflecting more of our values, we are reflecting more of society's values.

Bill Haslem, the former Republican governor of Tennessee, notes: "Christians are acting just like everyone else. We're just as likely to send a nasty message on the internet. We're just as likely to think we've won a battle because we have the most clever rhetoric on Twitter."[12]

---

10 But Jesus called them to Himself and said, "You know that the rulers of the Gentiles lord it over them, and those who are great exercise authority over them. Yet it shall not be so among you; but whoever desires to become great among you, let him be your servant. And whoever desires to be first among you, let him be your slave—just as the Son of Man did not come to be served, but to serve, and to give His life a ransom for many." Matthew 20:25-28

11 C. Peter Wagner, "I Like Donald Trump." *Charisma Magazine,* June, 10, 2016, *accessed* https://www. charismanews.com/politics/opinion/57707-c-peter-wagner-i-like-donald-trump

12 Emma Green, "The Evangelical Politician Who Doesn't Recognize His Faith—Or His Party: Bill Haslam, the former governor of Tennessee, is trying to figure out how religious Republicans got so extreme," *The Atlantic,* June 8, 2021, accessed https://www.theatlantic.com/politics/archive/2021/06/bill-haslam-trump-evangelicals/619101/

He also notes that Christians "in the public square" are not likely to be described as "pure, peaceable, and gentle."[13]

Unfortunately, there are far too many instances that support his observations.

We have seen that exalting success over spirituality and competence over virtue[14] in the public square has had its costs.

As Gov. Haslam notes: "There have been a lot of people, particularly younger people, whom I've talked with who say, 'If that's what the Church is, then I don't really want to be a part of it.'"[15]

At the end of the day, the American Church is not sinking because we do not have enough political power; we are sinking because we are more focused on the storms (the attacks) than we are on Jesus.

This observation is not meant to cast doubt on the idea that culture can be transformed through the increased presence of the Gospel. However, to the extent that our strategies for transformation are "more disciples in the right place, the high places" regardless of their virtue, and to value success over spirituality to gain influence, we suggest it is time for different strategies.

A focus on placing more disciples in the high places has produced many Christians who occupy positions at the top of key areas of society, most visibly in politics. Yet, it seems

---

13 See, Green, "The Evangelical Politician Who Doesn't Recognize His Faith—Or His Party"

14 "kings do not have to be virtuous," See, Wallnau, Johnson, *Invading Babylon*, 57

15 Green, "The Evangelical Politician Who Doesn't Recognize His Faith—Or His Party

that all we have done is to intensify the nature of the culture war in America. And as Gov. Haslam notes, turned off some people to the Church in the process.

Moreover, as the Pew Research Center studies mentioned above show, fewer people, as a percentage of the American population, identify as Christian, and more people, as a percentage of the American population, identify as religiously unaffiliated.

Fighting fire with fire has not created cultural transformation. We cannot use the tools of the world to influence the world. We must rely on the weapons employed by our role model for revolutionary transformation, Jesus, our Lord, and Savior. His weapons are not carnal but mighty in God to the pulling down of strongholds.

We will do well to remember that our Lord gave us a commandment. "Love each other just as much as I have loved you," John 13:34.

We will do well to remember that our role model "did not come expecting to be served but to serve and give his life in exchange for the salvation of many," Matthew 20:28.

We will do well to remember that God has called us to "constantly love each other and be committed to serve one another," Galatians 5:13. And when we do remember, we will realize that the greatest weapon we have is unconditional love expressed through serving others.

To return to our analogy, we will stop sinking when we, like Peter, reach for the outstretched hand of Jesus and allow Him and His ways to lift us up.

Becoming Great examines, in various ways and in a variety of contexts, God's call on the American Church to love and serve others. It is a collection of essays that provide an alternative to the current strategy of shaping culture by striving for and exercising power and authority from the top of society's institutions.

Becoming Great is divided into a prologue and five parts:

The PROLOGUE gives the back story to why *Becoming Great* is a collection of essays rather than a book. It also helps to explain the meaning of the book's subtitle.

PART ONE is *Unconditional Love*. People will know us and our God by the unconditional love we have for them. Part One contains essays on:

✢ what unconditional love looks like in action,

✢ how leaders of churches in America can display unconditional love even more often

✢ the prophetic call that God has for leaders in the spheres of culture, and

✢ the role of the Church in influencing significant aspects of culture.

The goal of Part One is to suggest how we can influence others by loving them unconditionally.

PART TWO is *Loving Our Neighbors*. We must love one another and be united in the Body of Christ before we can love and unite others. Part Two contains two essays. The first essay emphasizes the importance of recognizing the Church as the Body of Christ with Jesus as the head. The second essay explains the concept of the Church in the Community. It builds on the concept of Church in the Marketplace. It recognizes that we can serve beyond the sanctuary on Sunday and beyond the workplace from Monday through Friday. We can serve our neighbors seven days a week. The goal of Part Two is to suggest how members of the Body of Christ, individually and collectively, can positively impact our spheres of influence.

PART THREE is *Loving Our Enemies.* What makes Christianity so powerful is not a call to love other Christians. It is Jesus' call for us to love others, including those who look, believe, and act differently than we do. Answering God's call to love even those who would regard us as enemies is what gives Christianity the power to change lives. The essays in Part Three examine what it means to love those who treat us differently and to love those who may regard us as enemies. The primary goal of Part Three is to help us overcome obstacles that make it difficult to love others.

PART FOUR is *Service Motivated by Christlike Love.* To give a well-worn phrase a makeover, we can serve without loving, but we cannot love without serving. Part Four contains essays that focus on transforming society through service. The first essay recognizes that Jesus is a perfect role model for transforming society. This recognition will cause us to be different, to think differently, and to act differently. Part of acting differently, as discussed in Part Four's second essay, is leading social impact movements to advance Kingdom culture in society. This essay describes a framework for that purpose. The third essay discusses what we can do as individuals to advance Kingdom culture in our sphere of influence. The goal of Part Four is to suggest ways that service motivated by love can make a difference in our society.

PART FIVE is *Being Made Perfect in Love*. The Apostle Paul says in Ephesians 4:16, "Every member has been given divine gifts to contribute to the growth of all; and as these gifts operate effectively throughout the whole body, we are built up and made perfect in love." The essays in Part Five ask us to think differently about how we approach ministry and who gets to minister. The goal of Part Five is to suggest ways to unleash even more people into service that benefits our society.

Becoming Great ends with a reminder of why we desire to transform culture in the first place: "We are ambassadors of the Anointed One who carry the message of Christ to the world, as though God were tenderly pleading with them directly through our lips. So we tenderly plead with you on Christ's behalf, 'Turn back to God and be reconciled to him.' For God made the only one who did not know sin to become sin for us, so that we might become the righteousness of God through our union with him." 2 Corinthians 5:20-21.

Part One

Unconditional Love

"I have never been so discouraged about our nation," said a well-known Christian leader in Charisma Magazine. "We are in dire straits. I believe that much of America's malady has been caused over the years by the establishment politics of both parties in Washington, D.C. How do we get out of this quagmire?"[16]

His answer is influence. And "the chief producer of influence," he said, is "not spirituality but success. The most successful people are the most influential."[17]

Apparently, millions of other Christians share this answer. As Ralph Reed, chairman of the Faith and Freedom Coalition, said about the 2016 presidential election: "For Christians who feel they are engaged in a great struggle for the identity of America—and fear that their side has been losing ground— the most important question is not whether [the candidate] believes in their cause, but whether he can win their wars."[18]

---

16 C. Peter Wagner, "I Like Donald Trump" *Charisma Magazine,* June 10, 2016, *accessed* https://www. charismanews.com/politics/opinion/57707-c-peter-wagner-i-like-donald-trump

17 Wagner, "I Like Donald Trump"

18 Tim Alberta, "Trump and the Religious Right: A Match Made in Heaven", *Politico,* June 13, 2017, accessed : https://www.politico.com/magazine/story/2017/06/13/trump-and-the-religious-right-a-match-made-in-heaven-215251

However, as Johnny Enlow wrote in *Seven Mountain Prophecy*: "*Godly* influence can only be gained by operating in the opposite spirit from that which rules the world"[19] (emphasis added).

No one epitomizes "the opposite spirit" more than Jesus. Here are Jesus' thoughts on power, i.e., influence.

> *"But Jesus called them to Himself and said, 'You know that the rulers of the Gentiles lord it over them, and those who are great exercise authority over them. Yet it shall not be so among you; but whoever desires to become great among you, let him be your servant. And whoever desires to be first among you, let him be your slave— just as the Son of Man did not come to be served, but to serve, and to give His life a ransom for many,'"* Matthew 20:25-28 (NKJV).

While most of us believe exercising "great authority" is the way to be influential, Jesus encourages us to serve. To become great, we must serve others.

The very notion by Christians that our "side" is losing, and we need, as Mr. Reed says, someone to win our wars is counter to the teaching of Jesus. This notion implies that we are fighting an enemy.

Here are Jesus' thoughts on enemies:

> *"Your ancestors have also been taught 'Love your neighbors and hate the one who hates you.' However, I say to you, love your enemy, bless the one who curses you, do something wonderful for the one who hates you, and*

---

19 Johnny Enlow, *The Seven Mountain Prophecy: Unveiling The Coming Elijah Revolution* (Creation House. Lake Mary, FL, 2018), Kindle Edition, location 163

respond to the very ones who persecute you by praying for them. For that will reveal your identity as children of your heavenly Father. He is kind to all by bringing the sunrise to warm and rainfall to refresh whether a person does what is good or evil. What reward do you deserve if you only love the loveable? Don't even the tax collectors do that? How are you any different from others if you limit your kindness only to your friends? Don't even the ungodly do that? Since you are children of a perfect Father in heaven, become perfect like him," Matthew 5:43–48.

The opposite spirit from that which rules the world includes love and service.

Becoming Great advocates that Godly influence comes through serving others. But not just serving others but serving others motivated by Christlike love. As Pastor Bill Johnson wrote in *Invading Babylon*: "The Church is sometimes known for its willingness to serve, but usually with well-meaning spiritual agendas as the ultimate goal. ... As pure and noble as it may seem to us as believers, it is manipulative to the world, and ... The world can smell it a mile away but selfless, i.e., Christlike, service."[20] "It is serving for the benefit of another. It is the kind of a servant whom the world welcomes."[21]

Part One focuses on serving others motivated by Christlike love, i.e., Christlike service. It contains the following essays:

"Transforming Love" is an eight-part blog series on how the Church can do even more to display Christlike love.

---

20 See, Wallnau, Johnson, *Invading Babylon,* 25

21 Ibid, 26

"Seven Letters to the Leaders of Churches in America"
encourages leaders in the areas of Christlike love,
righteousness, church, culture, ministry, transformation,
transforming cities and nations.

"Seven Scrolls to the Leaders in the Spheres of Culture" is
a prophetic download I received from the Lord to share
with leaders in seven spheres of culture.

The final essay is a white paper on the role of the Church
in impacting society.

We will begin with Jesus' new commandment, to love
others as much as He loves us.

Chapter One
Transforming Love

"So I give you now a new commandment: Love each other just as much as I have loved you. For when you demonstrate the same love I have for you by loving one another, everyone will know that you're my true followers," John 13:34-35 (NKJV).

Chapter One is a call for leaders to:

❖ love others unconditionally,

❖ love without litmus tests, and

❖ stop using excuses (e.g., hate the sin, love the sinner; speak the truth in love) for why we do not love our enemies, bless those who curse us, do good to those who hate us, and pray for those who despitefully use us.

It contains an eight-part blog series on unconditional love.

PART 1
_____

When a lawyer asked Him, which is the great commandment in the law? *"Jesus said to him, 'You shall love the Lord your God with all your heart, with all your soul, and with all your mind.' This is the first and great commandment. And the second is like it: 'You shall love your neighbor as yourself.' On these two commandments hang all the Law and the Prophets,"* Matthew 22:37-38 (NKJV).

In John 13:34-35 (NKJV), Jesus gives His disciples a new commandment: *"That you love one another; as I have loved you, that you also love one another. By this all will know that you are My disciples, if you have love for one another."*

Yet, we seem to underappreciate that the Great Commission mandate in Matthew 28:19-20 to teach nations all that Jesus commanded us includes His commands to love: love God, love our neighbors as ourselves, and love one another as He has loved us.

To fulfill the Great Commission, we must transform our current view of love. I'm not saying we need to transform love itself, but we need to transform our mindset about love.

What do I mean?

Firstly, we give ourselves excuses not to love. Secondly, we don't understand that love is more than something we feel. It is more than something we do. Love is a vital part of who we are.

We will tackle those issues in Part Two.

PART 2

One of the first verses I committed to memory is I John 4:8 (KJV), *"He that loveth not knoweth not God; for God is love."*

One of the first songs I ever learned contained the lyrics (as I was taught to sing them), "Yes, Jesus loves me! Yes, Jesus loves me! Yes, Jesus loves me! For the Bible tells me so."

I spent most of my "Christian walk" being blessed by the truth that God is a God *of* love and that He loves us.

It's only relatively recently that I have come to recognize the truth that God *is* love. What a revelation! It transforms scripture, such as the "love chapter," I Corinthians 13.

This revelation helps me to see verses such as I Corinthians 13:1-3 differently (NKJV). It is true that:

> *Though I speak with the tongues of men and of angels, but have not love, I have become sounding brass or a clanging cymbal. And though I have the gift of prophecy, and understand all mysteries and all knowledge, and though I have all faith, so that I could remove mountains, but have not love, I am nothing. And though I bestow all my goods to feed the poor, and though I give my body to be burned, but have not love, it profits me nothing.*

Since God is love, it can be said that:

> Though I speak with the tongues of men and of angels, but have not *God*, I have become sounding brass or a clanging cymbal. And though I have the gift of prophecy, and understand all mysteries and all knowledge, and though I have all faith, so that I could remove mountains, but have not *God*, I am nothing. And though I bestow all my goods to feed the poor, and though I give my body to be burned, but have not *God*, it profits me nothing.

The recognition that God *is* love helps me to receive even more fully the blessings represented by the attributes of God:

> *God* suffers long and is kind; *God* does not envy; *God* does not parade itself, is not puffed up; does not behave rudely, does not seek its own, is not provoked, thinks no evil; does not rejoice in iniquity, but rejoices in the truth; bears all things, believes all things, hopes all things, endures all things. *God* never fails.

Wow! What a loving God we serve!

But then there is that pesky new commandment in John 13:34 (NKJV): *"That you love one another; as I have loved you, that you also love one another,"* reminding us that our blessings are not just about us.

We will explain what we mean in Part 3.

PART 3

What an incredible revelation to understand even more fully that God not only loves us He *is* love. This means:

> *God* suffers long and is kind; *God* does not envy; *God* does not parade itself, is not puffed up; does not behave rudely, does not seek its own, is not provoked, thinks no evil; does not rejoice in iniquity, but rejoices in the truth; bears all things, believes all things, hopes all things, endures all things. *God* never fails.

Jesus' new commandment that we love one another as He loves us reminds us that our blessings are not just about us.

Fortunately, God has equipped us for the great purpose of loving others as Christ loves us. His word tells us that we are made in the image and likeness of Him and that in Him, we live and move and have our being. We are His offspring (Genesis 1:26; Acts 17:28). If God is love, so, too, are we.

As R. Keith Whitt says: "Love is the greatest and purest essence of who a person is."[22]

Since God is love and we are His created beings, this means *we* suffer long and are kind; *we* do not envy; *we* do not parade ourselves, are not puffed up; do not behave rudely, do not seek our own, are not provoked, think no evil; do not rejoice in iniquity, but rejoice in the truth; bear all things, believe all things, hope all things, endure all things. *We* never fail.

What would our civil discourse, social media posts, and political activities be like if we understood that these behaviors are the tangible fruit of love?

Love also expresses itself in service. *"Little children, let us stop just saying we love people; let us really love them, and show it by our actions,"* I John 3:18 (TLB).

This realization puts into an even better context scripture like Ephesians 2:10 (TLB), *"It is God himself who has made us what we are and given us new lives from Christ Jesus; and long*

---

22 R. Keith Whitt, "What Does It Mean That God's Love Is Unconditional? *Bible Study Tools*," September 21, 2019, accessed https://www.biblestudytools.com/bible-study/topical-studies/the-unconditional-love-of-god.html

ages ago he planned that we should spend these lives in helping others," and James 2:14-17 (TLB), *"Dear brothers, what's the use of saying that you have faith and are Christians if you aren't proving it by helping others? ... So you see, it isn't enough just to have faith. You must also do good to prove that you have it. Faith that doesn't show itself by good works is no faith at all—it is dead and useless".*

Knowing that *we* are love and that our service to others flows out of our very identity should help us to live out Jesus' greatest challenges to us. We get to discuss those challenges in Part 4.

PART 4

God is love. We are made in the image and likeness of Him. In Him (love), we move and breathe and have our being. Thus, we are love. Because love expresses itself in service to others, this means we were born to serve.

When Jesus issued a new command to love one another as He loves us, it was not the only time He asked us to love as a way of distinguishing us from the rest of the world.

Check out Matthew 5:43-48 (TLB):

> *"There is a saying, 'Love your friends and hate your enemies.' But I say: Love your enemies! Pray for those who persecute you! In that way you will be acting as true sons of your Father in heaven. For he gives his sunlight to both the evil and the good, and sends rain*

on the just and on the unjust too. If you love only those who love you, what good is that? Even scoundrels do that much. If you are friendly only to your friends, how are you different from anyone else? Even the heathen do that. But you are to be perfect, even as your Father in heaven is perfect."

Wow! That's a tough one!

But if followers of Christ, those to whom He gave the Great Commission, are to have any hope of discipling nations, this is where it starts.

For decades Christians have been part of what we call the culture wars. More recently, we have become more active in the political arena. We have used the typical weapons of warfare in these culture wars—electing the "right" politicians, nominating the "right" judges, passing the "right" referendums.

The result? We elected a president who was supported by the vast majority of white evangelical Christians. He nominated, and the Senate confirmed three "pro-life" justices to the United States Supreme Court. And he signed an executive order that provides some protections for preachers to express their opinions about political matters from their pulpit.

But have we changed culture or just gotten better at using the world's weapons?

The best way to win the culture wars is not to fight them in the first place—more on that next.

PART 5

If we are to truly change the culture to reflect Kingdom values and Kingdom principles, we must remember that the weapons of our warfare are not carnal (political, legislative, judicial) but mighty in God for pulling down strongholds. See 2 Corinthians 10:4.

If we are to truly change the culture to reflect Kingdom values and Kingdom principles, we must follow Jesus' new commandment and love others as He loves us. Of all the other Kingdom values we display in our culture, the Kingdom value that has the most impact is love.

> *"Now here is what I am trying to say: All of you together are the one body of Christ, and each one of you is a separate and necessary part of it. Here is a list of some of the parts he has placed in his Church, which is his body: Apostles, Prophets—those who preach God's Word, Teachers, Those who do miracles, Those who have the gift of healing; Those who can help others, Those who can get others to work together, Those who speak in languages they have never learned. Is everyone an apostle? Of course not. Is everyone a preacher? No. Are all teachers? Does everyone have the power to do miracles? Can everyone heal the sick? Of course not. Does God give all of us the ability to speak in languages we've never learned? Can just anyone understand and translate what those are saying who have that gift of foreign speech? No, but try your best to have the more important of these gifts. First, however, let me tell you about something else that is better than any of them!"* I Corinthians 12:27-31 (TLB).

The Apostle Paul is, of course, talking about love. Each of us, with our gifts, is a necessary part of the Body of Christ. How we exercise those gifts makes a difference:

> *"If I had the gift of being able to speak in other languages without learning them and could speak in every language there is in all of heaven and earth, but didn't love others, I would only be making noise. If I had the gift of prophecy and knew all about what is going to happen in the future, knew everything about everything, but didn't love others, what good would it do? Even if I had the gift of faith so that I could speak to a mountain and make it move, I would still be worth nothing at all without love. If I gave everything I have to poor people, and if I were burned alive for preaching the Gospel but didn't love others, it would be of no value whatever."* I Corinthians 13:1-3 (TLB).

Because God is love and love is at the heart of His greatest commandments, I believe love is His (and thus, our) greatest weapon for discipling nations.

We cannot change American culture by using the culture's instruments of change. To paraphrase Albert Einstein, we can't change a situation by continuing to play by the rules that created it.

If we love others as Jesus loves us, we can change cultures. We can disciple nations. But much of our conduct these days does not reflect Christlike love.[23]

---

23 See, for example, this quote from a renowned Christian leader: "I couldn't care less about a leader's temperament or his tone of his vocabulary. Frankly, I want the meanest, toughest son of a gun I can find. And I think that's the feeling of a lot of evangelicals. They don't want Casper Milquetoast as the leader of the free world." John Fea, Evangelical Fear Elected Trump, *The Atlantic*, June 24, 2018, accessed https://www.theatlantic.com/ideas/archive/2018/06/a-history-of-evangelical-fear/563558/

What is Christlike love? We will answer that in Part 6.

PART 6

What is Christlike love? It is unconditional love. It is love without litmus tests. Christlike love is not based on our approval, our agreement, or our acceptance. Nor does it require us to approve everything, agree with everything, or accept everything.

Of course, we will encounter things of which we do not approve. We must not forsake love when we express our disapproval.

We will encounter opinions with which we disagree. We must not forsake love when we express our disagreement.

We will encounter circumstances that we just can't accept. We must not forsake love when we decline to accept them.

Christlike love does not focus on outcomes or results; otherwise, our love would be determined based on what happens next.

Christlike love sees needs and meets needs; otherwise, love is limited by our feelings and our moods.

How do we display love in the face of so many challenges?

We must remember that it's not just that love:

❖ suffers long and is kind,
❖ does not envy,

✤ does not parade itself,

✤ is not puffed up,

✤ does not behave rudely,

✤ does not seek its own,

✤ is not provoked,

✤ thinks no evil,

✤ does not rejoice in iniquity, but rejoices in the truth, and

✤ bears all things, believes all things, hopes all things, endures all things.

We must also remember that love *never* fails. Thus love:

✤ *always* suffers long and is kind,

✤ *never* envies,

✤ *never* parades itself,

✤ is *never* puffed up,

✤ *never* behaves rudely,

✤ *never* seeks its own,

✤ is *never* provoked,

✤ *never* thinks evil,

✤ *never* rejoices in iniquity,

✤ *always* rejoices in the truth, and

✤ *always* bears all things, believes all things, hopes all things, endures all things.

Our challenge is to remember that love is not just something we express, though we must express it. Love is also part and parcel of our identity. Paul says that love never fails, which means that when we love, we never fail.

Love is the greatest and purest essence of a person, and its proper expression brings fulfillment.[24]

We express love because of who we are, not because that's what the circumstances call for. And this seemingly impossible task is possible because we can do all things through Christ (love), who strengthens us. See Philippians 4:13.

So, what gets in the way of displaying Christlike love even more often? We will answer that next.

PART 7

What gets in the way of our display of Christlike love? We do.

It seems counterintuitive, but how we express our view of what it means to be a Christian can get in the way of our display of Christlike love.

For example, loving the sinner but hating the sin seems so Christlike. We have heard this phrase so often, some of us think this is a Bible verse. It is supposed to mean I hate what you are *doing*, but I love *you*.

If this is so, then I would love *you* regardless of *your sin*. I would never treat you less favorably than anyone else because of *your sin*.

But do I?

Adultery is a sin. Fornication is a sin. If I treat the fornicator differently from the adulterer, will the fornicator

---

24   Whitt, "What Does It Mean That God's Love Is Unconditional?"

believe that I love the sinner but hate the sin? Or is it more likely the fornicator will believe that I hate him? If I think it is okay to cater an event for married adulterers, but I refuse to cater an event for a cohabitating couple because they are not married, am I focusing on the sin (sex outside of marriage) or the sinner?

Would Jesus have treated the woman caught in adultery differently if she had been caught in fornication?

Let me quickly add that loving the sinner (that's each one of us because each one of us sins) does not require us to treat everyone the same all the time, but it does make it more likely that we will treat people similarly in similar circumstances.

Another phrase we have made into a verse is "speaking the truth in love." We use this "verse" most in two circumstances.

Firstly, we tell ourselves that no matter how unpleasant, we would want someone to correct the error of our ways.

Secondly, we say that we love people so much we don't want to see them go to hell. So, I'm going to tell them the truth about their behavior.

But unconditional Christlike love is always kind, never behaves rudely, does not seek its own, and thinks no evil. Thus, speaking the truth in love is not an excuse for speaking in an unloving way.

As one commentator observes: "The Bible instructs us to confront a brother or sister whenever we believe them to be sinning (2 Timothy 4:2), but too often our response is akin to bludgeoning others into submission, then justify our actions as, 'speaking the truth in love' ... we disguise our hasty words and harsh measures as loving rebuke."[25]

How do we solve this? How do we get out of our own way? We will discuss this next time.

PART 8

How do we overcome the roadblocks, some of them self-imposed, that interfere with our desire to display Christlike love?

Identity.

As mentioned earlier, God is love. We are made in His image and likeness. We are His sons and daughters. We move and breathe and have our being inside of Him. If He is love, so are we.

Love is not just something we do. Love is an essential part of our identity.

We must love from a place of our own identity. There's a saying, "No matter where you go, there you are." When we understand that a vital part of our identity is love, love is not dependent on the circumstances, the situation, or another person. We love because that's who *we* are.

---

25   Ryan Duncan, "Do You Know How To Speak The Truth In Love?" *Crosswalk.Com*, July 19, 2017, accessed https://www.crosswalk.com/blogs/christian-trends/do-you-know-how-to-speak-the-truth-in-love.html

It's the answer to that tough question. How do we follow Jesus' command in the Sermon on the Mount to love our enemies, bless those who curse us, do good to those who hate us, and pray for those who spitefully use us and persecute us?

We don't love them, bless them, do good to them, and pray for them based on who *they* are. We love them based on who *we* are.

My parents raised my brother and me to be polite. When we were younger, we would race to see who could open the door for our mother first. Being polite is part of who I am today. I recall a colleague of mine saying, "I've never met anyone with so many manners in my life!"

I am not polite to people based on who they are. Nor must people "earn" polite behavior from me. I am polite to people based on who *I* am. In other words, my politeness is unconditional.

When we realize that our love is part and parcel of our identity, we will be better able to display Christlike love even more often.

We suffer long and are kind; we do not envy; we do not parade ourselves; we are not puffed up; we do not behave rudely, do not seek our own; we are not provoked, think no evil; we do not rejoice in iniquity, but rejoice in the truth; we bear all things, believe all things, hope all things, and endure all things. We are love!

Help us, Lord!

Chapter Two

Seven Letters to the Leaders of the Churches in America

INTRODUCTION

In his book, *The Church in the Workplace*, Peter Wagner declared, "The Great Commission's biblical goal is nothing short of social transformation."[26]

"Our best top-level Christian leadership has been involved with this in city after city across America," he said. "[And] God has been providing incredible new tools for getting the job done."[27]

But despite these tools and even though social transformation has been "high on our priority lists" since 1990, "we cannot point to a single city in America that has been transformed."[28]

On the contrary, research shows that fewer Americans identify themselves as Christian,[29] and America, as

---

26 C. Peter Wagner, *The Church in the Workplace: How God's People Can Transform Society* (Regal Books, Ventura, CA 2006), 48

27 Wagner, *The Church in the Workplace*, 48

28 Wagner, *The Church in the Workplace*, 40

29 See, America's Changing Religious Landscape, *Pew Research Center*, May 12, 2015, accessed https://www.pewforum.org/2015/05/12/americas-changing-religious-landscape/

a country, is becoming more hateful.[30] Despite the efforts of many Christian leaders, American society looks less like— rather than more like—the Kingdom of Heaven on earth.

In fact, there is evidence that society has more influence on us than vice versa.

Many Christians rejoiced when a pro-life, conservative candidate was elected President. There was further rejoicing when he appointed three pro-life judges to the Supreme Court. But, as one White House staffer observed, "proximity to power does strange things even to pastors and ministers."[31]

He noted that some members of the President's faith advisory council engaged in the same "undermining" and "backbiting" that was evident with others close to the President.[32]

The fact that America, by some measures, is becoming less Christian even as Christian leaders gain unprecedented access to the highest levels of government illustrates the wisdom of heeding the Apostle Paul. He urged us in Romans 12:2 to not be conformed to this world.

Instead, he urged us to be transformed by the renewing of our minds.

---

30 "The number of hate crime incidents reported to the FBI increased about 17 percent in 2017 compared with the previous year, according to the Uniform Crime Reporting (UCR) Program's annual *Hate Crime Statistics* report." Hate Crime Statistics Released: Report Shows More Departments Reporting Hate Crime Statistics, *FBI News*, November 13, 2018, accessed https://www.fbi.gov/news/stories/2017-hate-crime-statistics-released-111318

31 Ed Stetzer, "Cliff Sims, the 'Team of Vipers,' and His Views of the President's Faith Advisors (Part 2)", *Christianity Today*, February 6, 2019, accessed https://www.christianitytoday.com/edstetzer/2019/february/cliff-sims-team-of-vipers-and-faith-inside-white-house-part.html

32 Stetzer, "Cliff Sims, the 'Team of Vipers,' and His Views of the President's Faith Advisors (Part 2)"

Transforming ourselves is essential if we are to transform society. To transform ourselves, we must do more than think differently from the rest of society—we must think differently, period.

What follows is a series of letters to the Body of Christ in America, in particular, its leaders. The letters seek to transform our thinking to better position the Body of Christ to transform society. Within the context of seven topics, they set forth how the Kingdom of God can be advanced and American society changed for the better.

The place to start is with a definition of transformation. The meaning of the word *"transformation"* as used in these letters is *"a process of profound and radical change that results in a new way of thinking, a new direction, and an entirely different level of effectiveness."*

But to what end? A new way of thinking and a new direction that brings about what? If the goal of the Great Commission is to bring about social transformation, what does social transformation look like?

I would suggest that the end result of social transformation is glory to God. What we do to bring about social transformation hastens the day when *"the earth will be filled with the knowledge of the glory of the Lord as the waters cover the sea,"* Habakkuk 2:14 (NKJV).

Pastor Eric Moore of Summit Worship Center in Austin, Texas, defines glory as the manifestation of God's holiness. *"You are glorious,"* sang Moses to the Lord. *"Because of Your holiness."* Exodus 15:11 (GW).

Understanding that God created us for His glory (Isaiah 43:7) and recognizing that we do good works to bring Him glory (Matthew 5:16) highlights the importance of Pastor Eric's insight. "How we treat people should manifest (reveal, display, make known) the glory (holiness) of God."

If we can transform ourselves into a people that treat others in a way that manifests the holiness of God, we will become a society full of the knowledge of the glory of God.

Transforming ourselves into such a society starts in the house of the Lord. That's why the audience for these letters is leaders of churches in America. It begins with how we can tangibly live out Jesus' commandment to love others as He loves us and teach others to do the same.

The first goal of the letters is to be part of what God is already doing on the earth to bring radical change to the Body of Christ in America. This transformation will take us in a new direction and to an entirely new level of effectiveness.[33]

The second goal of the letters is to model Jesus' new commandment to love others as He loves us. I hope that the letters model this love by sharing content in a way that is "incredibly patient, gentle, consistently kind, and never stops believing the best of others."[34]

---

33 In order to reach the first goal, the letters quote other commentators to (a) highlight some of the reasons why a profound and radical change must take place in the Body of Christ to bring about transformation and (b) share some of the profound and radical thinking that others are already doing to bring transformation to pass.

34 In order to reach the second goal, I have adopted an approach that is designed to resist the temptation that we all share of evaluating the message by evaluating the messenger. Thus, some direct quotes are set forth without explicit attribution to the author. My goal is to mitigate the conclusion that I am commenting about the character of the author rather than commenting about the content of the quote.

A LETTER ON CHRISTLIKE LOVE

To the Leaders of the Churches in America:

You have heard it said by Christian leaders that Christians in leadership who do not support President Trump are "moronic" and "stupid." You have heard it said by other Christian leaders that President Trump is "greedy, bloated, bitter, violent, self-centered."

But the Apostle John encourages us: *"Beloved, let us [unselfishly] love and seek the best for one another, for love is from God; and everyone who loves [others] is born of God and knows God [through personal experience]. The one who does not love has not become acquainted with God [does not and never did know Him], for God is love. [He is the originator of love, and it is an enduring attribute of His nature]"* 1 John 4:7-8 (AMP).

When we make comments that are not loving; when we defend actions and comments that are not loving; when we defend those who are not displaying Christlike love, how well are we representing the Father's unconditional love? Are we instead presenting a God that others perceive as unloving?

People cannot see our Father in Heaven, but they can see us. And when they see us and hear us, what conclusions are they likely to draw about our Father? That He is a judgmental God or a loving God? A condemning God or a saving God? A fearsome God or a compassionate God?

We shall know a tree by its fruit. If we are the fruit of the Father, what do our actions say about Him?

We live in a time when political opinions seem to dominate our social landscape, yet we refer to politics as "a dirty business."[35]

As followers of Christ, we can't disciple a nation by "doing dirt." Shouldn't we be teaching others how to love rather than allowing them to teach us how to be successful at "a dirty business"?

Wouldn't it be better if we were known by the love we have for others rather than the love we have for our political positions?

Dearest Leaders: *"Anyone can say, 'I love God,' yet have hatred toward another believer. This makes him a phony, because if you don't love a brother or sister, whom you can see, how can you truly love God, whom you can't see?"* 1 John 4:18-20.

"So, I give you now a new commandment: Love each other just as much as I have loved you. For when you demonstrate the same love I have for you by loving one another, everyone will know that you're my true followers" John 13:34-35.

My brothers and my sisters, many people look to us to see the Father's love demonstrated in real and tangible ways. When they see us, my prayer is that they will see us:

✤ loving our enemies,

✤ blessing those who curse us,

✤ doing good to those who hate us, and

✤ praying for those who would despitefully use us and persecute us.

---

35 Marko Joensuu, "Prophecy as propaganda: the Trump prophecies as political persuasion," *Mentoring Prophets*, December 2, 2012, accessed http://www.mentoringprophets.com/2016/12/prophecy-as-propaganda-trump-prophecies.html

May we greet everyone we encounter, not just our brethren. May we be kindly affectioned toward everyone, not just those who are kindly affectioned toward us. May we esteem all others more highly than we esteem ourselves, not just our like-minded friends.

May we love others the way our Father in Heaven loves us. Then perhaps more Americans will become acquainted with and changed by the God of love.

Grace and peace,

A Fellow True Follower of Christ

A LETTER ON RIGHTEOUSNESS

To the Leaders of the Churches in America:

You have heard it said, "We must call upon God to change the situation ... there must be a shift in the courts."[36]

But the Apostle Paul said: *"Yet we know that a person is made right with God by faith in Jesus Christ, not by obeying the law. And we have believed in Christ Jesus, so that we might be made right with God because of our faith in Christ, not because we have obeyed the law. For no one will ever be made right with God by obeying the law"* Galatians 2:16 (NLT).

If this is true of "the law of Moses," how much more valid is it for man's law?

---

36 Cathy Irvin, "Righteousness Exalts a Nation", *CBN*, accessed January 14, 2019, https://www1.cbn.com/devotions/righteousness-exalts-nation

During the confirmation hearings for Supreme Court Justice Brett Kavanaugh, there were Christians who emphasized the importance of his confirmation. Other Christians stressed the importance of denying his confirmation.[37]

Both sides prayed for righteousness. For one side of this debate, we needed prayer to ensure that righteousness did not "fall by the wayside in our judicial system." For the other side, prayer was needed to support "righteous resistance to bring down, or at least cripple, systemic racial and gender inequality."[38]

Both sides of the debate looked to the judicial system to produce or protect righteousness.

Indeed, for decades Christians of all "political stripes" have been focused on shaping elections, legislation, and propositions so that the "right" people would be elected to office or appointed to the bench. We hoped to produce a righteous nation through the passage of "righteous" laws interpreted by "righteous" judges.

Proverbs 14:34 says righteousness exalts a nation. It would seem that many of us believe that casting a vote has more power than living out our beliefs. Many of us believe that the judicial system will do more to bring about righteous behavior than reconciling sons and daughters with their Heavenly Father.

A nation is not made righteous through its political and judicial systems but by a people who become the righteousness of God through Jesus Christ.

---

37 See, Barbara Williams Skinner, "The Power of Prayer and Righteous Resistance", *Sojourner*, October 2, 2018, accessed https://sojo.net/articles/power-prayer-and-righteous-resistance

38 Skinner, "The Power of Prayer and Righteous Resistance"

If we had to become righteous through our own efforts, we would never get there. If we had to obey the law to become righteous, we would fall short. Without Jesus, we *cannot* become righteous. Without faith, our quest for righteousness is nothing more than a religious duty. It is through our faith that we are saved by grace, not by works.

God's grace does not mean we should do away with laws and regulations that help govern society and protect the health and well-being of its citizens. However, as Ambassadors for Christ, we prioritize our ministry of reconciliation more than our efforts to elect particular candidates. As one former White House aide said, "It's important to remember that the gospel matters more than politics."[39]

As this former aide said in an interview about his experiences, "The evangelist who leads one person to Christ on the weekend just did more than the most successful politician in the world. That's certainly not intended to discount the importance of policy issues for Christians, but sharing the gospel is certainly the most important thing."[40]

Dearest Leaders: *"The mature children of God are those who are moved by the impulses of the Holy Spirit. And you did not receive the 'spirit of religious duty,' leading you back into the fear of never being good enough. But you have received the 'Spirit of full acceptance,' enfolding you into the family of God. And you will never feel orphaned, for as he rises up within us, our spirits join him in saying the words of tender affection, 'Beloved Father!'"* Romans 8:14-15.

---

39 Ed Stetzer, Cliff Sims, 'Team of Vipers,' and Faith Inside the White House - Part 3, *Christianity Today*, February 13, 2019, accessed https://www.christianitytoday.com/edstetzer/2019/february/cliff-sims-team-of-vipers-faith-inside-white-house-part-3.html

40 Stetzer, *'Team of Vipers,' and Faith Inside the White House - Part 3*

Because we did not receive the spirit of religious duty, let us not impose that spirit on others. Let's share with others what we did receive, the Spirit of full acceptance.

To echo the words of Apostle Paul, if we find our righteousness in the faith of God and not in our works, why do we require people to live by works? See Galatians 2:14. *"For by the works of the law no flesh shall be justified"* Galatians 2:16 (NKJV).

Let's spend even more time as Christ's Ambassadors helping people attain righteousness through Jesus and less time legislating morality. *"Surely we don't need to speak further about the foolishness of trying to be saved by being good"* Hebrews 6:1 (TLB).

May we love others the way Jesus loved us by helping them to become the righteousness of God in Him. Then, perhaps, our collective righteousness will exalt our nation.

Grace and peace,

A Fellow Ambassador of Christ

A LETTER ON CULTURE

To the Leaders of the Churches in America:

You have heard it said that there is an "us" (the moral, conservative Christians to whom this nation really belongs), and then there is a "them" (in this case, liberal secularists whose sole objective is to undermine all biblical values).[41]

But the Apostle John said: *"Dear friends, let us practice loving each other, for love comes from God and those who are loving and kind show that they are the children of God, and that they are getting to know him better. But if a person isn't loving and kind, it shows that he doesn't know God—for God is love."* 1 John 4:7-9 (TLB).

There is a dividing line in America that has been called "the culture wars." Many Christian leaders are working hard to win this so-called war.

Unfortunately, every war needs an enemy. Battles must have an "us" and a "them." For "us" to win, "they" must lose. While it is true that Jesus talked about "the evil" and "the good," and "the just" and "the unjust," He did so to make a point. God makes His sun rise on and sends His rain to both.

Of course, we will treat people differently because we are uniquely different and occupy different circumstances. But following Jesus' example, we should not distinguish between people by loving some but not others, by treating one person with civility but not another.

For decades, "us" vs. "them" language has been dominant in American politics. This language has seeped into much of the dialogue when faith and politics intersect. Creating ideological "enemies" may be an effective way to galvanize supporters, but it's a terrible way to preach the Gospel.

---

41   Jesse Carey, "The Problem with Fighting a Christian Culture War", *Relevant*, January 8, 2015, accessed https://www.relevantmagazine.com/culture/problem-fighting-christian-culture-war/

Even if we consider our ideological opponents as actual enemies (which probably isn't the most productive starting point for winning them over), name-calling, baiting, or antagonizing isn't just ineffective. It's not biblical.

The other downside to viewing culture in "us" versus "them" terms is we make it about us, not God. Jesus did not call us to disciple nations by teaching the nations *our* commands but by teaching nations what Jesus has commanded us.

Dearest Leaders: *"You see, we don't go around preaching about ourselves. We preach that Jesus Christ is Lord, and we ourselves are your servants for Jesus' sake."* 2 Corinthians 4:5 (NLT).

Moreover, *"Speak blessing, not cursing, over those who reject and persecute you. Celebrate with those who celebrate, and weep with those who grieve. Live happily together in a spirit of harmony, and be as mindful of another's worth as you are your own. Never hold a grudge or try to get even, but plan your life around the noblest way to benefit others. Do your best to live as everybody's friend. Beloved, don't be obsessed with taking revenge, but leave that to God's righteous justice"* Romans 12:15-19.

The "world" behaves uncivilly, at best, toward those who regard it as an enemy. It returns evil for evil. It fights fire with fire. When we do the same, we are not the salt of the earth or the light of the world.

We are salt when we love even those who treat us as enemies and when we pass up opportunities to pay back evil for evil. When we, instead, conquer evil by doing good, we bring a light that drives out darkness. We win the culture war by not participating in it.

As Abraham Lincoln asked, "Do I not destroy my enemy when I make him my friend?" When there is no enemy, there is no war.

We can transform culture when we preach that Jesus Christ is Lord and we become servants for Jesus' sake. That is when we can help America know the glory of God.

Grace and peace,

A Fellow Servant for Jesus' Sake

A LETTER ON THE CHURCH

To the Leaders of the Churches in America:

You have heard it said, "conservative Christians have the right—and the responsibility—to take dominion over all aspects of life, including the government."[42]

But Jesus said, *"The rulers of the Gentiles lord it over them, and those who are great exercise authority over them. Yet it shall not be so among you; but whoever desires to become great among us, let him be a servant."* Matthew 20:25 (NJKV).

We know that Genesis 1:28 (NKJV) reads: *"Then God blessed them, and God said to them, 'Be fruitful and multiply; fill the earth and subdue it; have dominion over the fish of the sea, over the birds of the air, and over every living thing that moves on the earth.'"*

---

42 Dominionism And Democracy, *Church & State*, October, 2011 accessed https://www.au.org/church-state/october-2011-church-state/featured/dominionism-and-democracy

And we know that from one interpretation of this verse has emerged a theology called The Dominion Mandate. The common-sense definition of dominion conjures up images of one group controlling others. Indeed, the Hebrew word used for "dominion" in that verse, *radah*, means "to have dominion, rule, dominate."[43] Moreover, some have aligned the Seven Mountain Strategy[44] with this theology to advocate the position that Christians should serve God by "taking dominion of whatever mountain on which God has placed them." [45]

Not surprisingly, it is a theology some people have not received well. It has been called "wrong and dangerous."[46]

Who wants to be ruled or dominated by someone else? On the other hand, what follower of Christ would interpret the commandments to love God and to love others as a call to dominate others?

So then, how do we reconcile a Dominion Mandate theology with a God who calls on us to esteem others more highly than we esteem ourselves, to love others by serving others, and to be great by becoming a servant?

Johnny Enlow reminds us that "the Kingdom of God comes in freedom, and the order it brings is an inside-out

---

43 Strong's Hebrew Lexicon (KJV) s.v. *H7287 – radah*, accessed April 2, 2019 https://www. blueletterbible.org//lang/lexicon/lexicon.cfm?Strongs=H7287&t=KJV

44 aka the seven spheres of culture: "Each of the seven mountains represents an individual sphere of influence that shapes the way people think." See, Wallnau, Johnson, *Invading Babylon*, 54. These spheres are – arts & entertainment (including sports), business/economics, education, family, government/politics, media, and religion.

45 C. Peter Wagner, *On Earth As It Is In Heaven: Answer God's Call To Transform The World* (Regal Books, Ventura, CA 2012), 148

46 Dominionism – Dominion Theology, *Be Watchful*, accessed April 2, 2019 https://bewatchful.org/ dominionism-dominion-theology/

order, not an outside-in order. We must watch how we use dominion terminology and make sure that we are at no time shifting toward order by means of imposition. God has always had the power to do in a mere instant what He needs to have accomplished. Yet He has chosen to endure the arduous process of winning over hearts and minds through love in order to accomplish His goals. As He is, so must we be in this world" (See, 1 John 4:17).[47]

As Os Hilman notes, we do not exercise dominion but influence. And "influence is a result of our love, humility, and obedience to God, not a goal to be achieved."[48]

Displaying greatness through servant leadership rather than lording authority over others is one way for followers of Christ to exercise godly influence.

As the Apostle Paul says, there is an even more excellent way.

"A new commandment I give to you," Jesus said. *"That you love one another; as I have loved you, that you also love one another. By this, all will know that you are My disciples, if you have love for one another"* John 13:34-35 (NKJV).

We may debate the meaning of the Dominion Mandate (dominion over all aspects of life, dominion over non-human forms of life, or dominion over the spiritual realm).

---

47 Johnny Enlow, *The Seven Mountain Renaissance: Vision and Strategy through 2050* (Whitaker House, New Kensington, PA 2015), Kindle Edition, location 618

48 Os Hillman, "Adam and Eve Were Given Dominion Over their World. Does that mean we can expect the same? No, not exactly," *Reclaiming the 7 Mountains of Culture,* accessed April 2, 2019 from http://7culturalmountains.org/apps/articles/default. asp?blogid=4347&view=post&articleid=77284&link=1&fldKeywords=&fldAuthor=&fldTopic=0

However, we cannot debate Jesus' command that His followers love and teach nations to love.

And when it comes to dominion, love makes all the difference.

Dearest Leaders: *"Love is large and incredibly patient. Love is gentle and consistently kind to all ... Love does not traffic in shame and disrespect, nor selfishly seek its own honor. Love is a safe place of shelter, for it never stops believing the best for others"* 1 Corinthians 13:4-7.

If we:

❖ influence people through loving relationships rather than through rules;

❖ exercise influence rather than exert dominion in the roles we occupy; and

❖ disciple, equip, and send others to do the same perhaps we can fill America with a Christlike love that subdues evil by overcoming it with good.

Grace and peace,

A Fellow Disciple of Jesus

A LETTER ON MINISTRY

To the Leaders of the Churches in America:

You have heard it said that it's the job of the pastors or elders to equip the saints for attending church regularly, protecting and preserving the gospel and the gospel's ministry in their church, discipling other church members, and sharing the gospel with outsiders.[49]

The Apostle Paul said: *"He himself gave some to be apostles, some prophets, some evangelists, and some pastors and teachers, for the equipping of the saints for the work of ministry, for the edifying of the body of Christ."* Ephesians 4:11-12 (NKJV).

For many of us, equipping the saints for the work of ministry means equipping them to work in our local church ministry. Edifying the Body of Christ means edifying the local church.

No doubt Jesus loves our local churches. He has "good works" for them to perform. No doubt Jesus loves the Church at large, i.e., the Body of Christ. As we just read, He has given what we refer to as five-fold gifts to edify it.

Jesus also loves the nations, and He commissioned His disciples to teach nations all that He commanded us to do.

To carry out this Great Commission, we must understand Ephesians 4:11-12 in its fullness. According to Dick and Dr. Arleen Westerhof, a better understanding of these verses will cause a radical change in our thinking.

In *New Perspectives on Apostolic Leadership,* they wrote: "God is restoring the truth that apostles, prophets, evangelists, pastors, and teachers are meant to equip believers for the works of service (Eph. 4:11-12)."[50]

---

49 See, Jonathan Leeman, "Your 7 Job Responsibilities as a Church Member", *The Gospel Coalition*, February 3, 2015, accessed https://www.thegospelcoalition.org/article/your-7-job-responsibilities-as-a-church-member/

50 Bruce Cook, *Aligning with the Apostolic, Vol. 4: Apostles and Apostolic Movement In The Seven Mountains of Culture.* (Kingdom House Publishing. Lakebay, WA, 2012)

"No longer will it just be 'the anointed man or woman of God' who gets to minister. All of God's saints get to participate in God's Kingdom. This is going to require a radical change in how apostolic leaders think and act. Making this change, however, is imperative. If we do not, we will not see the Kingdom of God manifesting in and transforming our nations as God intended."[51]

We must understand that our purpose as leaders is to equip God's saints to serve because that's what ministry is, serving others. To disciple nations, this service must extend beyond the walls of the local church.

Through leaders like Ed Silvoso, we understand that we must minister (serve) in the marketplace. We must also minister (serve) beyond the marketplace. Leading businesses, schools, media companies, governmental agencies, etc., means serving others, not lording our authority over others.

We must also minister (serve) in our communities. Loving our neighbors as ourselves includes meeting the needs of our neighbors when we can.

Dearest Leaders: *"Every believer has received grace gifts, so use them to serve one another as faithful stewards of the many-colored tapestry of God's grace. For example, if you have a speaking gift, speak as though God were speaking his words through you. If you have the gift if serving, do it passionately with the strength God gives you, so that in everything God alone will be glorified through Jesus Christ. For to him belong the power and the glory forever throughout all ages!"* 1 Peter 4:10-11.

---

51 Dick and Dr. Arleen Westerhof, "New Perspectives on Apostolic Leadership", *Aligning with the Apostolic, Vol. 4*, Kindle Edition, location 1220 & 1237.

God has blessed us with gifts. By His grace we are able to use those gifts as He intended, to equip others. We can equip other church members, those who attend our ministry seminars, and also one another.

Through our desire to serve others motivated by love, we help others determine how God wants them to use *their* gifts to serve others.

Through His power and anointing, we equip others for the work of the ministry; not just church ministry, not just our ministry, but *the* ministry.

By God's grace, may we be faithful in our ministry, and may we help others do the same. As we edify the Body of Christ, perhaps we can also edify America.

Grace and peace,

A Fellow Minister

A LETTER ON BEING TRANSFORMED

To the Leaders of the Churches in America:

You have heard it said that the chief producer of influence in the secular arena is not spirituality but success. The most successful people are the most influential.[52]

But the Apostle Paul said, "*Stop imitating the ideals and opinions of the culture around you but be inwardly transformed*

---

52 Wagner, "I Like Donald Trump,"

by the Holy Spirit through a total reformation of how you think" Romans 12:2.

Perhaps we can begin this act of reformation by rethinking the notion that we can transform the world by pursuing the world's definition of success. As followers of Christ, our spirituality remains the best way to influence others and to transform society.

Moreover, as one long-time ministry leader has observed: "If the existing church structures and ministry could have accomplished God's purpose for His church, it would have been fulfilled by now."[53]

Many church leaders believe that if we are going to transform society, we must adopt Kingdom—rather than local church—thinking.

"The Holy Spirit is strongly speaking to the churches to initiate a paradigm shift from being church-centered to being Kingdom-centered. The central issue behind this shift is how we *think*."[54]

I believe the Holy Spirit has initiated another paradigm shift: from a Kingdom mindset to a transformation mindset. The central issue behind this shift remains how we think.

What is a transformation mindset? The transformation mindset implies a basic change of thinking that has little or no resemblance to past thinking regarding society's features.

---

53 Alain Caron, *Apostolic Centers, Shifting the Church, Transforming the World* (Arsenal Press. Colorado Springs CO, 2013), ii

54 C. Peter Wagner, *Changing Church: How God Is Leading His Church Into The Future* (Regal Books. Ventura, CA 2004)

The Church Mindset, the Kingdom Mindset, and the Transformation Mindset are not mutually exclusive, nor is one better or worse than the other two; in fact, they may operate simultaneously within the same sphere.

Dearest Leaders: Now that you have heard Christ's voice and learned from Him the truths concerning Himself, *"your attitudes and thoughts must all be constantly changing for the better. Yes, you must be a new and different person, holy and good. Clothe yourself with this new nature."* Ephesians 4:20-24 (TLB).

What if we no longer imitated the existing church structures and ministry and instead renewed our minds to bring about transformation? What if we adopted a transformation mindset?

What if we adopted a mindset that endeavored to:

❖ disciple nations by focusing on the nations;

❖ accomplish the work of the ministry by equipping everyone for ministry; and

❖ change people's lives by being among the people, loving them, and serving them?

Below I have set forth the major elements of the Transformation Mindset. For illustration, I have compared it to a Church Mindset and a Kingdom Mindset.[55]

---

55 I must give credit to Dr. Peter Wagner who produced a PowerPoint for Global Spheres that delineated the differences between churches and apostolic centers. (C. Peter Wagner, Apostolic Centers. *Glory of Zion*, accessed November 3, 2012 from https://gloryofzion.org/docs/Apostolic%20Centers_sm.pdf.) It is the primary source for what I have set forth below regarding the Church Mindset and the Kingdom Mindset. The basis of the Transformation Mindset was inspired by hearing Bob Hartley explain what God gave him regarding a Hope Mindset. (Bob Hartley and Michael Sullivant, The Hope Reformation Room — An Angelic Encounter, *1Soul 1Nation*, October, 2012, accessed from http://1soul1nation.blogspon. com/2012/10/bob-hartley-and-michael-sullivant-hope.html)

Many times, when we see side-by-side comparisons, such as the one below, there is a temptation to view one as better than the other. That is NOT the case here.

It takes intentionality to bring people to salvation and to disciple them. The Church Mindset brings that intentionality. It takes intentionality and a different mindset to equip saints for the work of ministry. The Kingdom Mindset brings that intentionality. Similarly, it takes intentionality and a different mindset to bring about the transformation of society. The Transformation Mindset brings that intentionality.

Or put another way: a Church Mindset is indispensable for saving souls, a Kingdom Mindset is indispensable for equipping saints for the work of ministry, and a Transformation Mindset is indispensable for replacing the current culture with a Kingdom Culture.

Church Mindset	Kingdom Mindset	Transformation Mindset
Preach the Gospel	Light of the World	The Glory & Presence of God
The Word of God	The Power of God	The Power of Hope in God
Salvation (personal)	Equip the Saints (for ministry)	Called by Love to Serve Others (to make His way known)
Personal Renewal	Body of Christ	Cities & Nations
Bring In (to the church)	Send Out (to the world)	Be Among (the people/ not of the people)
Retain Members	Release Saints	Help the Helpers
Pastor-Led	Apostle-Led	Hope Fueled, Love-Led
One Priest	Five-Fold Ministers	Every Person a Transformer

Church Mindset	Kingdom Mindset	Transformation Mindset
Care for Sheep	Mobilize the Army	Empower the People
Three-Fold Gifts	Five-Fold Gifts	Knowledge, Skills, Abilities

The three mindsets do not function in isolation, and they may operate in harmony when found within the same context.

A Transformation Mindset expands the Church Mindset (the territory in which we preach the Gospel.) It expands the Kingdom Mindset (the number of ways we share the Gospel). And it expands the group of people who are declaring the Gospel.

Surely, we can transform America when more ground is covered, more methods are employed, and when we deploy even more Ambassadors of Christ to reconcile people with their Heavenly Father. And isn't reconciling people to God one of the best ways to bring the Kingdom of Heaven to earth? Thanks be to God for this indescribable gift!

Grace and peace,

A Fellow Transformer

A LETTER ON TRANSFORMING CITIES AND NATIONS

To the Leaders of the Churches in America:

You have heard it said that "God's Word gives no commission to the church to fix the problems of the world."[56]

But Jesus said, *"'Don't you know? When you cared for one of the least important of these my little ones, my true brothers and sisters, you demonstrated love for me'"* Matthew 25:40.

Jesus came to seek and to save that which was lost in terms of salvation. He also came to bring us to wholeness. He came that we would have life and have that life more abundantly. Not just as individuals but as a community.

Jesus came to transform the world from one based on righteousness through the law to one focused on bringing the Kingdom of Heaven to earth.

However, as Anglican Priest and theologian John R. W. Stott said, "[T]he very notion that Christians can exert a healthy influence in the world should bring us up with a start. What possible influence could the people described in the beatitudes exert in this hard, tough world?"[57]

---

56 T.A. McMahon, "The Shameful Social Gospel", *The Berean Call,* October 1, 2019, accessed https://www.thebereancall.org/content/shameful-social-gospel-0?sapurl=Lys5MjZkL2xiL2xpLyt3dm44dWs4P2JyYW5kaW5nPXRydWUmZW1iZWQ9dHJ1ZSZyZWNlbnRSb3V0ZT1hcHAud2ViLWFwcC5saWJyYXJ5Lmxpc3QmcmVjZW50Um91dGVhHVnPSUyQnd2bjh1azg= January 14, 2019

57 R.W. Stott, *The Message of the Sermon on the Mount,* (InterVarsity Press, Downers Grove, IL 1978), 57

Yet Stott reminds us that Jesus did not shrink back from this "hard, tough world." Jesus knew there would be persecution, but He viewed it as the Church's calling not only to overcome evil with good but to serve others[58]. Service includes giving food to the hungry, providing drink for the thirsty, giving shelter to the homeless, furnishing clothes for the naked, and visiting the sick and the imprisoned (See, Matthew 25:31-40).

Not only are followers of Christ called to fix the world's problems by serving others, but we are also called to overcome evil in the earth by serving our enemies (*"If your enemy is hungry, buy him lunch! Win him over with kindness."* Romans 12:20).

Dearest Leaders: *"Your ancestors have also been taught 'Love your neighbors and hate the one who hates you.' However, I say to you, love your enemy, bless the one who curses you, do something wonderful for the one who hates you, and respond to the very ones who persecute you by praying for them. For that will reveal your identity as children of your heavenly Father. He is kind to all by bringing the sunrise to warm and rainfall to refresh whether a person does what is good or evil. What reward do you deserve if you only love the loveable? Don't even the tax collectors do that? How are you any different from others if you limit your kindness only to your friends? Don't even the ungodly do that? Since you are children of a perfect Father in heaven, you are to be perfect like him"* Matthew 5:43-48.

Jesus calls us to be different. As Stott noted, our ability to influence society depends on our being different from the

---

58 See, Stott, *The Message of the Sermon on the Mount,* 57

rest of society.[59] The Sermon on the Mount, he says, "is built on the assumption that Christians *are* different, and it issues a call to us to *be* different."[60]

Our most significant difference is following Jesus' "new" commandment: to love others as He has loved us, i.e., Christlike love.

Love is the foundation of transformation. Episcopalian Bishop The Most Reverend Michael Curry quoted Charles Marsh in *The Beloved Community* to observe, "Jesus began the most revolutionary movement in human history: a movement grounded in the unconditional love of God for the world and a movement mandating people to live that love, and in so doing to change not only their lives but the very life of the world itself."[61]

---

59 See, Ibid

60 Ibid, 63

61 Michael Curry, "Make love the way — Presiding Bishop Michael Curry preaches at royal wedding." *Anglican Communion News Service.* May 5, 2018, accessed from http://www.anglicannews.org/news/2018/05/make-love-the-way-presiding-bishop-michael-curry-preaches-at-royal-wedding.aspx

Chapter Three

The Lord's Seven Scrolls to the Seven Mountains of Culture

I am not particularly prophetic. In fact, in an activation session, after Bill Hamon taught conference attendees how to hear the voice of God, I shared an impression with my activation partner that was not accurate.

But two days later, as I was walking back to my apartment after a workout, I received a series of prophetic words about each of the seven mountains of culture.[62] I hurried home and wrote them down.

After sharing inaccurate prophetic words a couple of days before, why would I trust that what I was "hearing" was from the Lord?

In short, the activation session taught me to trust what I was hearing. What I heard during the activation session did not make any sense to me. Unless I was correct,

---

62 aka the seven spheres of culture: "Each of the seven mountains represents an individual sphere of influence that shapes the way people think." See, Wallnau, Johnson, *Invading Babylon,* 54. These spheres are – arts & entertainment (including sports), business/economics, education, family, government/politics, media, and religion.

sharing it was going to be embarrassing. The back-and-forth negotiation with God about whether to share my impression ended with me sharing it. The lesson: to be brave enough to run the risk of being wrong. To trust what I heard if I thought what I heard was from God.

Besides, just because what I shared two days previously did not make sense (yet) to my partner did not mean that Bill Hamon had done a poor job of activating the prophetic in me.

Thus, two days later, when I was writing down what I heard in my head, I trusted that I was hearing from the Lord. To hold myself accountable, I also added the scripture that supported the word God had given me for each of the seven mountains (as President Reagan famously said, trust but verify).

The following is what I heard that morning from the Lord:

My mountain is an upside-down mountain. It is an upside-down pyramid, not a triangle because I sent my Son to serve not to be served (*And whoever desires to be first among you, let him be your slave—just as the Son of Man did not come to be served, but to serve, and to give His life a ransom for many.* Matthew 20:27-28).

BUSINESS

Open the scroll to the mountain of commerce. You call it the business mountain because the object is to make money, but it is about commerce so that they who have can trade with those who have not. I would not have some in abundance and some in lack. It is about an economics of mutuality *(For I do not mean that others should be eased, and you burdened; but by an equality, that now at this time your abundance may supply their lack, that their abundance also may supply your lack—that there may be equality. As it is written, "He who gathered much had nothing left over, and he who gathered little had no lack."* 2 Corinthians 8:13-15).

ARTS & ENTERTAINMENT

Sing a new song, write a new play, pen a new script that is not TO Me or FOR Me but Me THROUGH YOU. I will put a new song, a new play, a new script in your heart so that men, women, and children will see your good work and glorify Me *(He has put a new song in my mouth. Praise to our God; Many will see it and fear, And will trust in the Lord.* Psalm 40:3 [NKJV]; Matthew 5:16).

MEDIA

Media is nothing but a message. For the message to be pure, the messenger must be pure (of motive). Purify your heart so that the pure message that I give to you will remain pure as it is delivered and received. *(As I urged you when I went into Macedonia—remain in Ephesus that you may charge some that they teach no other doctrine, nor give heed to fables and endless genealogies, which cause disputes rather than godly edification which is in faith. Now the purpose of the commandment is love from a pure heart, from a good conscience, and from sincere faith, from which some, having strayed, have turned aside to idle talk, desiring to be teachers of the law, understanding neither what they say nor the things which they affirm.* I Timothy 1:3-7).

FAMILY

In this age, you think of nuclear families (one household of parents and children), but do you not know that all my sons and daughters belong to one family? All are connected; what happens to one family happens to all. Build and enrich My family so that your family will be blessed, for We are One *(Now you are no longer strangers to God and foreigners to heaven, but you are members of God's very own family, citizens of God's country, and you belong in God's household with every other Christian.* Ephesians 3:19 [TLB]).

GOVERNMENT

You see government as a way to rule; I see government as a way to serve; great governments act on behalf of people, to bring people into their destinies, not their "don't do these"; to enrich through service, not enslave through regulation *(Jesus called them to Himself and said, "You know that the rulers of the Gentiles lord it over them, and those who are great exercise authority over them. Yet it shall not be so among you; but whoever desires to become great among you, let him be your servant. And whoever desires to be first among you, let him be your slave.* Matthew 20:25-27).

EDUCATION

I will write my laws on the tablets of your hearts; education is not about acquiring information but learning of Me and My ways and My statutes; let Me place my statutes in your hearts for they are not grievous (*"The law of the Lord is perfect, converting the soul; The testimony of the Lord is sure, making wise the simple; The statutes of the Lord are right, rejoicing the heart; The commandment of the Lord is pure, enlightening the eyes."* Psalm 19:7-8 [NKJV]; *"This is the covenant that I will make with them after those days, says the Lord: I will put My laws into their hearts, and in their minds I will write them,"* Hebrews 10:16 [NKJV]*).

RELIGION

What is man that he is but a little lower than the angels; religion is nothing more than learning, understanding, discerning, and living out your proper place in My creation and with Me. You are my sons and daughters, and I long to be with you (*Now all of us, whether Jews or Gentiles, may come to God the Father with the Holy Spirit's help because of what Christ has done for us. Ephesians 2:18 [TLB]*).

OPEN THE SCROLLS TO MY HEART AND LEARN OF ME.

Chapter Four

The Role Of The Church In Bringing Cultural Transformation

BACKGROUND

If it is true that "lasting cultural transformation only occurs when the Gospel infiltrates every aspect of society,"[63] and if it is true, as some Christian leaders believe, that the Church has "lost its cultural influence,"[64] then what should the Church be doing differently to bring the Gospel to every sphere of culture?

This white paper examines the role of the Church in influencing cultural transformation. It highlights two important commissions for which it is uniquely equipped.

---

63 "Each of the seven mountains represents an individual sphere of influence that shapes the way people think." See, Wallnau, Johnson, Invading Babylon, 54. These spheres are – arts & entertainment (including sports), business/economics, education, family, government/politics, media, and religion.

64 Joseph Mattera, "8 Reasons Why the Church Lost the Culture Wars in North America," *Joseph Mattera*. December 15, 2020; retrieved from https://josephmattera.org/reasons-church-lost-culture-wars-2/

Firstly, God calls on His Church to serve others motivated by "a high measure of love." When its behaviors are rooted and grounded in love, e.g., loving our neighbors through selfless service, the Church helps to transform society.[65]

Secondly, God calls on His Church to establish Kingdom culture. It does so by 1) making disciples of leaders, influencers, and others in each sphere of culture, 2) equipping those disciples to advance Kingdom culture and to make more disciples, and 3) "sending" those disciples into their respective spheres of influence to replace the current culture with Kingdom culture.[66]

CONTEXT

We begin the paper by setting forth the following perspectives of key terms:

The "Body of Christ" (many members, one body with Jesus as the head) is present on all seven mountains. Unlike the Church (big C), it is not an institution.

The "Church" (big C) refers to the Ekklesia. It is defined as that institution assembled in the name of Jesus and composed of people who sustain a certain relationship to Him, i.e., the *assembled* people of God. It "resides" on the Religion Mountain, as do the smaller subsets of

---

65 See, Wallnau, Johnson, *Invading Babylon*, 25

66 Note: When referencing disciples in general the area of focus will be the seven mountains; when referencing individual disciples the reference will be to their sphere of influence.

the Church, the *"local church" (small c)*, but some of its activities are performed on, and impact, the other six mountains.[67]

The *"Seven Mountains"* represent the main cultural spheres of society. These spheres are—arts and entertainment (including sports), business/economics, education, family, government/politics, media, and religion. Each sphere of culture shapes the way people think.[68]

The *"Religion Mountain"* is the sphere of culture that shapes our view of spirituality. The "Church" and the "Religion Mountain" are NOT used interchangeably in this paper.

For purposes of this paper, we will use the following definitions:

✤ "the Church" (THE institution): the followers of Christ assembled together,

✤ "the local church": (AN institution): local churches are the subsets of the larger institution,

✤ "the Body of Christ": the unassembled followers of Christ,

✤ "the Seven Mountain Strategy": transforming culture by impacting the seven spheres of culture with the Kingdom of God; and

✤ "the Religion Mountain": the sphere of culture which shapes our view of spirituality.

---

67 Similarly, universities "reside" on the Education Mountain but perform activities on, and impact, other mountains.

68 See, Wallnau, Johnson, *Invading Babylon*, 54

THE CURRENT VIEW OF THE IMPACT OF THE CHURCH TO IMPACT CULTURE

One proponent of the Seven Mountain Strategy stated: "The Church lacks cultural power because it focuses on changing the world from within the Church mountain rather than releasing the Church into the marketplace to leaven all seven mountains."[69]

He continues: "The goal isn't to pull a convert out of the world and into a church, as we so often do. The goal is to be the Church that raises up disciples who go into all the world."[70]

THE ROLES OF THE CHURCH ON THE SEVEN MOUNTAINS:

A Proposal

The two comments cited above suggest two roles of the Church on the seven mountains. Firstly, the Church must move beyond its established place on the mountain of Religion to serve others on all seven mountains. Secondly, the Church should "raise up disciples" who make, equip, and send other disciples who make, equip, and send disciples who establish Kingdom culture in their sphere of influence.

Let's discuss both of these critical roles.

---

69 See, Wallnau, Johnson, Invading Babylon, 65

70 Ibid

Releasing The Church To Serve

When Pastor Bill Johnson spoke of societal transformation in *Invading Babylon*, he stated, "The goal is the transformation of society itself by invading the systems of the city in order to serve." But the key, he said, is "serving for their benefit, not ours."[71]

He continued, "When we set aside our religious agendas to make others a success, we have learned the Kingdom mindset and have become a part of the transformation movement."[72]

He gave the following example, "when we volunteer in our local school to help the principal succeed, then we've crossed the line into territory seldom visited by the Church. It is serving for the benefit of another. It's that kind of a servant whom the world welcomes. The amazing bonus is you also end up influencing the school in ways you never thought possible, including bringing people to Christ."[73]

That's a great example, but can serving really "leaven" or impact culture? Yes, it can.

As Barbara and Steve Chua, senior pastors of Life As One Church in Claremont, California, recounted in a Transform Our World Ekklesia Excelerator General Assembly[74], showing up simply to serve motivated by Christlike love can make a difference.

---

71 Ibid, 25

72 Ibid

73 Ibid, 26

74 See, ©Ed Silvoso, Transform Our World Ekklesia Excelerator

The Chuas visited the local continuation high school[75] to pray for the school's administrators. Regular prayer times led to the more active involvement of the members of Life As One, including mentoring some of the school's students. As a result, foul language was reduced, class attendance and classroom behavior improved, and the percentage of the student population who graduated increased.

Unfortunately, as Pastor Bill points out, this kind of selfless service is "territory seldom visited by the Church." "Christians are notorious for trying to take over schools through political maneuvering," he said. "It may work from time to time, but it is neither the way of the Kingdom nor will it prevail. There is a better way."[76]

Like the Chuas, we must find and utilize that better way. We must "visit" selfless service much more often. The Chuas have demonstrated that "when we set aside our religious agendas to make others a success, we have ... become a part of the transformation movement."[77]

Moreover, the Chuas have given us a blueprint. Start by showing up simply to pray with the leaders of businesses, institutions, networks, associations, performing arts

---

75 A continuation high school is an alternative for students "who haven't already graduated and are at risk for not graduating. The purpose of continuation high schools is to give students, who may have family, drug or other problems such as depression, an alternative to complete their education." See, Sheri Cyprus, "What is a Continuation High School?" *Practical Adult Insights,* February 05, 2021, retrieved https://www.practicaladultinsights.com/what-is-a-continuation-high-school.htm

76 Wallnau, Johnson, *Invading Babylon,* 26-27

77 Ibid, 25

centers, studios, government agencies, etc.[78] Then be open to invitations and opportunities to serve in ways that benefit others, not ourselves nor our "religious agendas."

As Pastor Bill states: "The Church is sometimes known for its willingness to serve, but usually with well-meaning spiritual agendas as the ultimate goal. It almost sounds blasphemous but serving simply to get people saved is a religious agenda. As pure and noble as it may seem to us as believers, it is manipulative to the world and is viewed as an impure service. The world can smell it a mile away."[79]

The more we release the Church to serve others (not our "well-meaning spiritual agendas") on each of the seven mountains, the more effective we become at transforming our society.

Raising up Disciples to Establish Kingdom Culture in Their Sphere of Influence

The second role performed by the Church on the seven mountains "is to be the Church that raises up disciples who go into all the world."[80]

This aspect of the Church's role is strikingly similar to the role many apostolic centers already play.

Because an apostolic center has been described as "a new structure for advancing God's kingdom culture to every

---

78 A gentle reminder: prayer has not been banned in schools nor does separation of church and state prevent prayer in public or government institutions. What has been banned is "state-sponsored" prayer.

79 Wallnau, Johnson, *Invading Babylon,* 25-26

80 Ibid, 65

sphere of influence in society and to every nation," the comparison is fitting.[81][82]

Another fitting comparison relates to the reason commentators believe the Church (big C) and the local church (little C) struggle to influence society. The Church (big C) lacks cultural power because it focuses on changing the world from within the Religion Mountain. This comment mirrors a comment made about the local church (little C), i.e., that the local church lacks influence because it focuses on changing its community from within the sanctuary.

In other words, the Religion Mountain is just another, much larger, expression of the sanctuary's four walls. And to the extent the Church's focus is primarily on what happens within those four walls, i.e., on the mountain of Religion, its effectiveness is limited.

Let me quickly add that some of what happens within the four walls of the sanctuary is so valuable as to be incalculable. But just as the local church should not be limited to what happens within the four walls of a sanctuary, the Church should not be limited to what happens on the mountain of Religion.

Nor should the Church limit itself to "religious activities." As C. Peter Wagner noted, even as we "pray harder, worship longer, fast more frequently, intensify spiritual

---

81 Che Ahn, "A New Wineskin", *Harvest Rock Church Blog*, retrieved https://harvestrock.church/new-wineskin/

82 Some of the characteristics of an apostolic center are: a) it is led by an apostle, b) it has apostles, prophets, evangelists, pastors, c) it makes disciples, d) it equips those disciples to serve others, e) it sends those disciples to serve others.

warfare, and live more holy lives," American society is "moving further and further away from Kingdom principles, not closer."[83]

As Dr. Wagner stated: "What the churches should do is to equip their workplace saints to function more effectively and to rise up to positions of influence in their mountains."[84]

And as it turns out, our local churches are in a unique position to do just that.

"Although the work of culture creation may take place outside the physical walls of a church building," Gabe Lyons says, "the local church creates a natural space where social networks of leaders, within all seven channels of culture, can work together towards a common goal. Nowhere else does this potential for synergy exist."[85]

In addition to being even more intentional about creating synergy among the cultural influencers in its midst, the Church should enthusiastically embrace activities apostolic centers already perform that impact culture.

In summary, those activities are to:

✤ Reconcile sons and daughters with their Heavenly Father,

✤ Make Disciples,

---

83 C. Peter Wagner, *This Changes Everything: How God Can Transform Your Mind And Change Your Life.* (Chosen Books. Bloomington, MN, 2013), 191-192

84 Wagner, *This Changes Everything,* 192

85 Gabe Lyons, "Cultural Influence: An Opportunity For The Church." *Comment.* March 1, 2008, accessed https://www.cardus.ca/comment/article/cultural-influence-an-opportunity-for-the-church/

❖ Equip Disciples, and

❖ Send Disciples

As we will discuss in more detail later, making disciples includes instilling biblical values, attitudes, and beliefs in reconciled sons and daughters of our Heavenly Father. Another part of making disciples is helping reconciled sons and daughters discover their gifts (whether they be ministerial [Ephesians 4:11-13], motivational [Romans 12:3-8], and/or spiritual [I Corinthians 12]).

When the Church helps people discover their God-given gifts, they are unleashing apostles, prophets, and pastors; discerners, healers, and miracle workers, as well as encouragers, teachers, and leaders into their calling and purpose.

Consider that:

❖ People with an apostolic gift are likely to be leading and influencing workgroups, professional associations, PTAs, trade guilds, etc.

❖ People with the gift of teaching are likely to be trainers, facilitators, classroom teachers, executive coaches, professors, dance instructors, daycare workers, athletic coaches, etc.

❖ People with the gift of administration are likely to be chief operating officers, executive secretaries, general managers, chiefs of staff, school administrators, producers, etc.

❖ People with the gift of leadership are likely to be chief executive officers, department heads, principals, union leaders, heads of PTAs, legislators, etc. And so on.

In other words, when the Church disciples artists and entertainers, business people, educators, marriage and family counselors, politicians, journalists, and ministry leaders to establish Kingdom culture in their sphere of influence, it contributes to cultural transformation.

To be sure, such transformation will happen initially in pockets. But over time, these pockets, whether small or large, will connect and intersect to create greater influence.

As Os Hillman said: "We are each called to become change agents in the sphere of influence God has called us to impact. As each of us does this, we reclaim the culture one person at a time, one industry at a time, one mountain at a time."[86]

And it starts with a Church that makes, equips, and sends Kingdom-minded disciples to fulfill their God-given assignments in each of the seven mountains.

Let's discuss these activities further.

RECONCILING SONS AND DAUGHTERS WITH THEIR HEAVENLY FATHER

I believe the first priority of any Kingdom-minded ministry, organization, or group in transforming culture is to reconcile sons and daughters with their Heavenly Father. So, while the primary focus of this white paper is on discipleship, our foundational role as Christ's ambassadors to be ministers of reconciliation is worth mentioning here.[87]

---

86 Os Hillman, "Impacting The 7 Mountains Of Culture: A New Move of God," *GodTV*, February 19, 2019; accessed https://godtv.com/impacting-the-7-mountains-of-culture-a-new-move-of-god/

87 See, 2 Cor. 5:17-21

MAKING KINGDOM-MINDED DISCIPLES WHO SERVE

A vital, more specific activity is making disciples. That is, to develop sons and daughters who have been reconciled with their Heavenly Father into learners, disciples, followers of Christ who learn the doctrines of Scripture and the lifestyle they require.[88]

It is important to note that making disciples is not just about teaching reconciled sons and daughters the Word of God but helping them to live the Word of God. It is the display of biblical values, attitudes, and beliefs that make the followers of Christ different. And we cannot make a difference in our respective spheres of influence unless we *are* different.

For example, leading differently.

"Kings and those with great authority in this world rule oppressively over their subjects, like tyrants. But this is not your calling. You will lead by a completely different model. The greatest one among you will live as the one who is called to serve others, because the greatest honor and authority is reserved for the one with the heart of a servant. For even the Son of Man did not come expecting to be served but to serve and give his life in exchange for the salvation of many." Matthew 20:25-28.

And leading for different reasons.

---

88 See, HELPS Word-studies (2001) Bible Hub, accessed https://biblehub.com/greek/3101.htm

As Pastor Bill Johnson said in *Invading Babylon*: "The effort by many believers to simply obtain positions of leadership is putting the cart before the horse. Servanthood remains our strong suit, and through service we can bring the benefits of His world into the reach of the common man."[89]

In fact, for the "seven realms of society" to come under the influence of the King, "the people of God [must] go forth to serve by bringing the order and blessing of His world into this one."[90]

The Church is uniquely qualified to make disciples who lead in a way that brings even more areas of culture under the influence of Kingdom values, attitudes, and beliefs.

In my experience, many local churches make disciples by holding Bible studies, Sunday School classes, and Kingdom institute courses.

To impact culture, I suggest the Church make disciples by utilizing the apprenticeship model to an even greater extent. It is a model that we see practiced throughout the Bible (Elijah and Elisha, Moses and Joshua, Paul and Timothy). In this discipleship model, a more experienced disciple helps a less experienced disciple "learn the doctrines of Scripture and the lifestyle they require" and instills biblical values, attitudes, and beliefs within them.

In the apprenticeship model, the disciple:

---

89 Wallnau, Johnson, *Invading Babylon,* 22
90 Ibid

❖ Learns from observing someone who knows the work as well as listening to lectures;

❖ Learns by doing as well as by completing lessons; and

❖ Learns how to do the Word as well as memorize the Word.

When the apprenticeship model is applied, it produces a Kingdom-minded disciple. And it also produces someone who is apostolic (more on the meaning of apostolic in this context later); someone who is even more capable of establishing Kingdom culture in her sphere of influence.

However, for the apprenticeship model to work, it needs experienced disciples who are good at employing it. Thus, two critical activities of the Church are to "make" Kingdom-minded disciples and train those disciples to make more disciples in their sphere of influence.

These Kingdom-minded disciples, in turn, make other disciples. And all of these disciples are focused on establishing Kingdom culture in their sphere of influence.

This brings us to the third activity we want to discuss, equipping disciples.

EQUIPPING KINGDOM-MINDED DISCIPLES *FOR* SERVICE

According to the Expositor's Bible Commentary, the Greek word for "equip" (as used in Ephesians 4:12) means "to prepare, to put right." But it is important to note that such "preparation is in order to [perform] the work of service." Thus, a vital activity of the Church is to equip Kingdom-minded disciples to serve in their sphere of influence.

Essential activities of the Church in this regard include preparing Kingdom-minded disciples to effectively a) share Kingdom values, attitudes, and beliefs and b) influence others to adopt them as well. Compared to other entities, the Church is uniquely qualified to do so.

Equipping Kingdom-minded disciples for the "work of service" includes preparing them to perform the good works which God has prepared in advance for them to do in their sphere of influence. Thus, the Church should support in any way it can people God has called to be performance artists, entrepreneurs, principals, family counselors, county supervisors, news editors, worship leaders, etc., as they seek to be excellent practitioners of their profession.

The combination of making Kingdom-minded disciples *who* serve and equipping Kingdom-minded disciples *for* service is a powerful one so long as these Kingdom-minded disciples are sent to perform the good works for which they have been "made" and "equipped."

This brings us to the fourth activity, sending disciples.

SENDING EQUIPPED KINGDOM-MINDED DISCIPLES *TO* SERVE

The Church "sends" disciples to individual spheres of culture in much the same way the Roman empire sent military leaders (i.e., "apostles") to bring Roman culture to foreign territories. It was important to establish Roman culture to ensure the territory's citizens did not rebel against Rome in an attempt to "revert back to their old identities." Thus, the apostle was sent to make sure the territory's culture became Roman.[91]

Since the goal is "lasting cultural transformation," the Church's role in sending Kingdom-minded disciples to transform their sphere of influence is critical.

If we define culture as shared values, attitudes, and beliefs, and if we define transformation as a change in the essential nature and character of a thing, then cultural transformation is brought about by a lasting change in the nature and character of its shared values, attitudes, and beliefs.

This type of change cannot be legislated, regulated, or policed. We must influence people to adopt it. As Johnny Enlow put it, "It's about influence, not domination."[92] "Influence is the by-product of having favor. ... True Godly favor is that which comes by carrying a high measure of love. That high measure of

---

91   Johnny Enlow, *The Seven Mountain Renaissance: Vision and Strategy Through 2050*. (Whitaker House: New Kensington, PA, 2015), 88

92   Enlow, *The Seven Mountain Renaissance*, 41

love will manifest in actions that are attractive to people of good will."[93]

The Church influences cultural transformation by making, equipping, and sending Kingdom-minded disciples who change the essential nature and character of their sphere of influence. Through influence gained by serving others motivated by "a high measure of love," these disciples can replace society's current set of values, attitudes, and beliefs with Kingdom values, attitudes, and beliefs.

The Church "sends" disciples in several different ways:

✤ *Releasing*: encouraging disciples to serve where they have been called rather than automatically recruiting them to serve the local church;

✤ *Aligning*: helping disciples to exercise their spiritual and ministry gifts within the context of their secular environments not just in church and in ministry environments;

✤ *Ordaining and commissioning*: spiritually empowering apostles and other five-fold ministers to operate in their gifting in their sphere of influence,

✤ *Supporting*: engaging in intercessory prayer, providing wise counsel, and supplying other support for disciples as they perform good works/acts of service in their sphere of influence.[94]

---

93 Ibid, 49-50

94 "Many Christians currently hold unique and influential positions throughout the seven channels of culture, but have never been supported by fellow believers." Gabe Lyons. Cultural Influence: An Opportunity For The Church. *Comment.* March 1, 2008, access https://www.cardus.ca/comment/article/cultural-influence-an-opportunity-for-the-church/

SUMMARY

In summary, the roles of the Church in transforming culture are to serve people motivated by Christlike love and to make disciples of God's people, equip them, and "send" them to establish Kingdom culture in their spheres of influence.

When it performs these roles to an even greater extent, we will no longer need to rely on a type of Cyrus who wields power and authority to influence culture. Instead, when we carry out God's "mandate to express His heart of love through every area of culture ... His way, the earth will rejoice!"[95]

---

95 Enlow, *The Seven Mountain Renaissance,* 41

Part Two

Loving Our Neighbors

"And the second is like unto it, you shall love your neighbor as yourself."

A lawyer then asked one of the most well-known questions in the New Testament, *"What do you mean by 'my neighbor'?"* Luke 10:29. In response, Jesus related one of the most familiar parables in the New Testament, the Good Samaritan.

He ended the parable by asking a question of His own: *"So, now, tell me, which one of the three men who saw the wounded man proved to be the true neighbor?"* Luke 10:36. The religious scholar responded, *"The one who demonstrated kindness and mercy."* Luke 10:37.

The goal of Part Two is to suggest how members of the Body of Christ, individually and collectively, can positively impact our sphere of influence. It starts by being "true neighbors." It includes expressing our love by serving others, even those who may not look like us, believe like us, vote like us, worship like us, etc.

To become a "true neighbor," the American Church must be different. Not only different from the rest of society but also different from the current version of itself. A gentle reminder: in the parable of the Good Samaritan, it was "church folk" who crossed to the other side of the road.

Part Two contains the following essays that advocate ways for the Church to be different:

Church: But Not As You Know It is an essay on taking a more expansive view of five terms that we use often—pro-life, pro-choice, pro-marriage, pastoring, and reconciliation. A more expansive view of each of these terms will allow us to demonstrate even more broadly and more deeply unconditional love to our neighbors.

Reformation of the Church is a white paper that asks us to see ourselves more as the Body of Christ than as THE Church.

Church in the Community is a white paper that builds on the concept of church in the workplace. It encourages us to see ourselves as part of God's Ekklesia twenty-four hours a day, seven days a week, in our communities as well as the marketplace. This concept is another opportunity for us to demonstrate that we are "true neighbors."

Chapter Five

Church — But Not As We Know It

According to a recent Pew study, 46 percent of registered voters say that life in America today is worse than it was fifty years ago "for people like them." When almost half of Americans say life is getting worse, not better, clearly something must be done.

As Christians, we can't keep doing what we've been doing and expect society to change. To make a difference, we must be different. Jesus said as much during His Sermon on the Mount: *"For if you love those who love you, what reward have you? Do not even the tax collectors do the same? And if you greet your brethren only, what do you do more than others? Do not even the tax collectors do so?"* Matthew 5:46-47 (NKJV).

One place to be different is defining some of the significant issues confronting society; how we define issues shapes how we approach them. We must begin to define them in a way that reflects the unconditional love of a Heavenly Father. He makes His sun to shine on all of us and sends His rain without distinction.

I propose a redefinition of five terms, not as a replacement for the current definitions but to incorporate an expanded role for "the Church," i.e., the imitators of Christ. Redefining these terms will result in a broader perspective that encompasses the unconditional love of Jesus.

Those five terms are:

Pro-Life: An expanded definition would include the Church's advocacy for programs that help make life better for people outside the womb. What if the Church established (or worked with others to provide) even more programs that equipped people to feed, house, and educate themselves, more programs that comforted the sick and the shut-in, and more programs that ministered to the imprisoned?

Pro-Choice: An expanded definition would include providing more viable choices for women who are considering abortion. What if the Church worked to open more pregnancy clinics and worked with organizations, including Planned Parenthood, that provide information on pregnancy and prenatal care? Such alliances would allow the Church to reach even more pregnant women about programs that will support their choice to keep their baby. More importantly, what if the Church did even more to support those programs?

Pro-Marriage: An expanded definition would include even more support for the institution of marriage. Such support would include an even greater focus on more pre-marital counseling and marital mentoring by happily married couples, not just pastors (see below). What if the Church focused even more intently on strengthening all marriages, not just "Christian" marriages?

Pastor (the verb): Even Christians tend to think of pastoring as ministry performed by a pastor. What if "to pastor" also meant to serve? What if even more of God's people pastored others in their sphere of influence? Pastoring would then take place everywhere, not just within the church walls. It would take place every day of the week, not just on Sundays.

Reconciliation: An expanded definition would include reconciling earthly parents with their earthly sons and daughters. What if the Church established and supported even more programs to strengthen families, facilitate adoptions, and help young mothers and fathers become even more emotionally and financially capable of caring for their children?

We would effect a difference that would make a difference if:

✤ pro-life also meant equipping people to live productive lives,

✤ pro-choice included providing viable alternatives to women considering abortion,

✤ pro-marriage also meant programs that reduced the divorce rate,

✤ pastoring included people ministering to those within their sphere of influence,

✤ reconciliation also meant bringing earthly parents into the same household as their earthly sons and daughters, and

✤ The Church embodied those definitions to serve people with unconditional Christlike love.

Chapter Six

Church Reformation: Not THE Church But HIS Church, The Body Of Christ

America, and indeed, many parts of the world, are facing challenges to its status quo: pandemic-driven public health orders, justice-driven calls for systematic changes, and partisan-driven divisiveness. Each of these challenges is causing massive disruption to our lives, livelihoods, and societal underpinnings, including but not limited to our religious, civic, business, educational, governmental, medical, and public safety institutions.

If there was ever a perception that American citizens shared values, that perception is under siege. Americans find themselves on opposite sides of issues that, a few years ago, would have brought the vast majority of us together. We would have agreed that:

❖ we should use all the tools at our disposal to eradicate a pandemic,

❖ we should condemn interference in our elections by a foreign country,

- police officers should be held accountable for misconduct, and

- looting is always a criminal offense.

Followers of Jesus *do* share values. We seek guidance from the same God. We read from the same Bible. We do our best to obey the same commands. Yet, our lives, livelihoods, and underpinnings also face challenges to the status quo. We, too, find ourselves on the opposite sides of issues. We are called to be one with each other and with our God, yet we are as divided as the rest of American society.

Recently, a student of mine made the following observation about the times in which we live: "Spirit-filled people all over are asking, 'What are the prophets saying about this Pandemic and Social Justice?'" She moved beyond that observation to remark perceptively, "It occurred to me that they should be asking, 'What are the Apostles saying we should do?'"

Good question, I thought. What *are* the apostles saying? That got me to praying. "Lord, what are you saying through those who are called as apostles? What are you saying to me?"

I prayed, meditated, and sought the heart of the Father. What I heard in my spirit was that the Lord is calling on us to relinquish our hold on the status quo so that we can embrace our identity as the Body of Christ, not *"The"* Church but *"His"* Church.[96]

---

96 I do not pretend that I am the only one who has heard this word. As related to me by one of my students, in Heidi Baker's message during a Revival Alliance Zoom call meeting this past April she shared that God asked her who she was several times. Her answers were about her ministry, her title, and what she does. But according to her, God wanted her to say that she is the Body of Christ, that we are the Bride of Christ. God is asking us during this time, "Are you a beautiful bride?" Are we being the hands and feet of Jesus?

This white paper suggests that reformation of the Church is needed if we are going to respond to the Lord's call. It explains what this reformation entails, describes the shifts required to bring it to pass, and finally, offers some thought starters about specific actions a reformed Church can take to transform society.

For our purposes, a summary definition of Church reformation is: changing the ways (methods of accomplishing a goal) and practices (activities performed repeatedly) of the Church while strengthening its fundamental values and principles.[97]

Central to this reformation is a fresh revelation of what it means to be His Body, the Body of Christ. The Apostle Paul has given us a wonderful description of the Body of Christ by comparing it to the human body:

> Just as the human body is one, though it has many parts that together form one body, so too is Christ. For by one Spirit we all were immersed and mingled into one single body; a body formed in the image of Christ, the head, closely joined together and constantly connected as one. Each member of the body has a unique function and has been given divine gifts to contribute to the growth of all. As these gifts operate effectively throughout the whole body, we are built up and made perfect in love. From: I Corinthians 12:12-14, Romans 12:4-5, Ephesians 4:15-16.

---

97 A grateful acknowledgement of Alain Caron, author of *Apostolic Centers,* and his definition of reformation from which this definition is derived.

As we gain a fresh revelation of what it means to belong to the Body of Christ, we may want to reconsider ways and practices that reinforce the notion of the Church as an institution, i.e., *The* Church.[98] We may instead want to embrace ways and practices that reflect our standing as members of *His* body. After all, institutions do not bring individuals to Christ; people do.

WHY CHURCH REFORMATION IS ESSENTIAL

To better understand why reformation of the Church in America is so essential, it is vital to recognize that our focus is not just on the Church; it also encompasses America itself.

Why? Because Jesus said so:

> *"All the authority of the universe has been given to me. Now go in my authority and make disciples of all nations, baptizing them in the name of the Father, the Son, and the Holy Spirit. And teach them to faithfully follow all that I have commanded you"* Matthew 28:18-20.

If the focus of Church reformation also includes discipling America, it makes sense to ask ourselves, how well are we doing at discipling our nation? Consider this two-question assessment: 1) To what extent is America obeying all that Jesus commanded His disciples to do? 2) To what extent is the American Church focused on pursuing The Great

---

98   References to the Church as an institution will be accompanied by an italicized *The*, as in *The* Church

Commission compared to one of its other focuses, winning the culture war?[99]

I would suggest the answer to both questions is: "to a small extent."

What do the answers suggest about the current state of the Church in America? More importantly, what do they suggest about its future?

In his 1963 "Letter From Birmingham Jail"[100], Dr. Martin Luther King, Jr., observed: "The contemporary church is so often a weak, ineffectual voice with an uncertain sound. It is so often the arch supporter of the status quo. Far from being disturbed by the presence of the church, the power structure of the average community is consoled by the church's often vocal sanction of things as they are."

To the extent this is true in 2020, and I would suggest it is,[101] what are the consequences if the Church does not change? In other words, why is Church reformation so essential? The words of Dr. King provide us with an answer.

"If the church of today does not recapture the sacrificial spirit of the early church," he wrote. "It will lose its

---

99 One Christian organization claims "that there is an "us" (the moral, conservative Christians who this nation really belongs to) and then there is a "them" (in this case, liberal secularists whose sole objective is to undermine all biblical values)." Jesse Carey, "The Problem with Fighting a Christian Culture War", *Relevant*, January 8, 2015, accessed https://www.relevantmagazine.com/culture/problem-fighting-christian-culture-war/

100 See, African Studies Center, University of Pennsylvania, accessed https://www.africa.upenn.edu/Articles_Gen/ Letter_Birmingham.html

101 Says Dr. Tony Evans, senior pastor of Oak Cliff Bible Fellowship in Dallas, Texas: "Our nation's ills are not merely the result of corruption or racism, although these are evil. Our troubles can also be traced directly to ineffective Christians." Praying and Seeking Real Change, *The Urban Alternative*, accessed from https://tonyevans.org/praying-and-seeking-real-change/

authentic ring, forfeit the loyalty of millions, and be dismissed as an irrelevant social club with no meaning for the twentieth century."[102]

Unfortunately, there are signs that this is happening. The results of Pew Research Center telephone surveys conducted in 2018 and 2019 show that 65 percent of American adults describe themselves as Christians, down twelve percentage points over the past decade. Meanwhile, the percentage of the population who describe their religious identity as atheist, agnostic, or "nothing in particular" increased by nine percentage points from 17 percent in 2009 to 26 percent.[103]

So then, how do we "recapture the sacrificial spirit of the early church"? One way is to reform the ways and practices of the Church so that they reflect, to an even greater extent, its most fundamental values and principles.

> *And there is something more important to God than all the sacrifices and burnt offerings: it's the commandment to constantly love God with every passion of your heart, with your every thought, and with all your strength — and to love your neighbor in the same way as you love yourself."* Mark 12:33.

The Church's most fundamental value is love, and one of its most fundamental principles is that God calls us to serve one another. By focusing on the Church's most fundamental values and principles, we can reform its ways

---

102 African Studies Center

103 See, "In U.S., Decline of Christianity Continues at Rapid Pace: An update on America's changing religious landscape," *Pew Research Center*, October 17, 2019, accessed https://www.pewforum.org/2019/10/17/in-u-s-decline-of-christianity-continues-at-rapid-pace/

and practices. We can do so in a manner that enables it to regain the sacrificial spirit necessary to disciple a nation.

But before we discuss how to bring Church reformation to pass, let's come to a common understanding (at least in this white paper) of what we mean by "Church" and what we mean by "Reformation."

WHAT WE MEAN BY CHURCH

Let's be clear about what we mean when we say "Church" reformation. We mean *His* Church, the Body of Christ, not *The* Church, not the institution many of us in America are trying to protect, as in, *The* Church is under attack.[104]

In describing it as His Church, our desire is not to offer a new definition of Church; instead, our desire is to re-embrace the original definition, "that institution which assembles in His name, and which is composed of people who sustain a certain relationship to Him, i.e., people in Christ."[105]

Paul's comparison of "people in Christ" to the human body is apt.[106] Both, unlike an institution, have life, and since all

---

104 Liberty Counsel Action website: accessed https://lcaction.org/detail/20200713your-church-is-under-attack

105 See, Abilene Christian Word Study, first accessed on August 9, 2018 from http://www.acu.edu/legacy/sponsored/restoration_quarterly/archives/1950s/vol_2_no_4_contents/ward.html

106 *Just as the human body is one, though it has many parts that together form one body, so too is Christ. For by one Spirit we all were immersed and mingled into one single body. And no matter our status—whether we are Jews or non-Jews, oppressed or free—we are all privileged to drink deeply of the same Holy Spirit.* I Corinthians 12:12-13

cellular life contains DNA[107], it makes sense to incorporate DNA into Paul's analogy.

We think of DNA as a distinguishing feature, as in DNA being used to rule out a person as a criminal suspect. And that is true of the Body of Christ as well. Jesus said the world would know us by the love we have for one another.[108]

However, DNA is also a unifying feature. We can connect distinct parts to one body, no matter how different they appear to the human eye. Our eyes, toes, ears, and hands, each of our body parts, contain the same DNA. So, it is with the Body of Christ. No matter how different we look from one another, we know we belong to the Body of Christ because we carry the same DNA as the other members of the Body.

Relying on the analogy of the human body given to us by Paul in 1 Corinthians 12, we can identify our unifying DNA as "the same Holy Spirit."[109] And what are the characteristics of this DNA? *"The fruit produced by the Holy Spirit within you is divine love in all its varied expressions: joy that overflows, peace that subdues, patience that endures, kindness in action, a life full of virtue, faith that prevails, gentleness of heart, and strength of spirit."* Galatians 5:22-23.

As His Church, the Body of Christ, we are united in the display of this "divine love in all its varied expressions." *"For the Lord God is one, and so are we,"* Ephesians 4:5.

---

107 See, DNA, *ScienceDaily*, accessed from https://www.sciencedaily.com/terms/dna.htm

108 *When you demonstrate the same love I have for you by loving one another, everyone will know that you're my true followers.* John 13:35

109 See, I Corinthians 12:12

THE DIFFERENCES BETWEEN THE CHURCH AND HIS CHURCH, THE BODY OF CHRIST

To illustrate the differences between *The* Church as an institution, and *His* Church, the living Body of Christ, with many members who carry the same DNA, I have chosen the intersection of race and religion. This intersection helps to bring into sharp relief the difference between an institution, which has not always been on "the right side of history,"[110] and members of the Body of Christ, who have on innumerable occasions shown "mutual concern" for other members.[111]

This is what former slave and abolitionist Frederick Douglass said about *The* Church:

> *But the church of this country is not only indifferent to the wrongs of the slave, it actually takes sides with the oppressors. It has made itself the bulwark of American slavery, and the shield of American slave-hunters.*[112]

This is what Mr. Douglass said about certain members of the Body of Christ in the same speech:

---

110 See, Terry Gross, "American Christianity Must Reckon With Legacy Of White Supremacy, Author Says," *NPR*, July 30, 2020, accessed https://www.npr.org/2020/07/30/896712611/american-christianity-must-reckon-with-legacy-of-white-supremacy-author-says

111 See, Adele Banks, "J. D. Grear Urges SBC to Retire Historic Gavel from Slaveholding Preacher," *Christianity Today*, June 10, 2020 accessed https://www.christianitytoday.com/news/2020/june/jd-greear-southern-baptist-convention-broadus-gavel-sbc.html

112 Frederick Douglass, "What to the Slave is the Fourth of July?", *The American Yawp Reader*, accessed https://www.americanyawp.com/reader/democracy-in-america/frederick-douglass-what-to-the-slave-is-the-fourth-of-july-1852/

Noble men may be found, scattered all over these Northern States, of whom Henry Ward Beecher of Brooklyn, Samuel J. May of Syracuse, and my esteemed friend on the platform, are shining examples; and let me say further, that upon these men lies the duty to inspire our ranks with high religious faith and zeal, and to cheer us on in the great mission of the slave's redemption from his chains.[113]

As a result, despite his views of *The* Church, Mr. Douglass ended his speech with hope:

Allow me to say, in conclusion, notwithstanding the dark picture I have this day presented of the state of the nation, I do not despair of this country. There are forces in operation, which must inevitably work The downfall of slavery. "The arm of the Lord is not shortened," and the doom of slavery is certain. I, therefore, leave off where I began, with hope.[114]

This is how Dr. King made the distinction between *The* Church and members of the Body of Christ in his "Letter from Birmingham Jail":

I commend you, Reverend Stallings, for your Christian stand this past Sunday in welcoming Negroes to your Baptist Church worship service on a nonsegregated basis. I commend the Catholic leaders of this state for integrating Springhill College several years ago. But despite these notable exceptions, I must honestly reiterate that I have been disappointed with the church.[115]

---

113 Frederick Douglass, "What to the Slave is the Fourth of July?"

114 Ibid

115 African Studies Center

Yet, Dr. King, like Mr. Douglass, had hope in God:

> *I hope the church as a whole will meet the challenge of this decisive hour. But even if the church does not come to the aid of justice, I have no despair about the future. ... We will win our freedom because the sacred heritage of our nation and the eternal will of God are embodied in our echoing demands.*[116]

When I think of *The* Church today, sometimes I, too, feel a sense of disappointment.[117]

However, like Mr. Douglass and Dr. King, when I take stock of what members of the Body of Christ are doing to advance the cause of righteousness and justice[118], I do not despair. I have hope in God.

To see members of the Body rather than an institution (or a stereotype or a generalization or my bias), I must be inwardly transformed by the Holy Spirit through a total reformation of how I think.[119] If we can reform how we think about the Church, we can understand the differences between *The* Church and the Body of Christ when it comes to:

---

116 Ibid

117 See, Leah MariaAnn Klett, "Evangelical seminary condemns Black Lives Matter movement, 'wokeness' ideology," *Christian Post,* August 20, 20, accessed https://www.christianpost.com/news/evangelical-seminary-condemns-black-lives-matter-movement-wokeness-ideology.html

118 I think about what is happening just within my own sphere: the group of ministers and their ministry teams who engaged with me in an extended dialogue about what their ministries could do to advance racial justice; the platform I was given as part of an extended focus on racial justice in the newsletter of an apostolic network with members in over 50 countries.

119 See, Romans 12:2

Who We Are

The Church is an institution with constitutional rights; the Body of Christ has many members with shared values.

> *I urge you, my brothers and sisters, for the sake of the name of our Lord Jesus Christ, to agree to live in unity with one another and put to rest any division that attempts to tear you apart. Be restored as one united body living in perfect harmony. Form a consistent choreography among yourselves, having a common perspective with shared values.* I Corinthians 1:10.

What We Are Trying To Accomplish

The Church is focused on winning a culture war; members of the Body of Christ are focused on discipling nations.

> *Then Jesus came close to them and said, "All the authority of the universe has been given to me. Now go in my authority and make disciples of all nations, baptizing them in the name of the Father, the Son, and the Holy Spirit. And teach them to faithfully follow all that I have commanded you."* Matthew 28:18-20.

How We View Our Brothers And Sisters

The Church takes an "us" versus "them" perspective; members of the Body of Christ have a mutual concern for members of the Body:

> *God has mingled the body parts together, giving greater honor to the "lesser" members who lacked it. He has done this intentionally so that every member would look*

*after the others with mutual concern, and so that there
will be no division in the body. In that way, whatever
happens to one member happens to all. If one suffers,
everyone suffers. If one is honored, everyone rejoices.*
I Corinthians 12:24-26.

How We View Our Neighbors

The Church fights for its liberty, members of the Body of
Christ consider their neighbors:

> *So, now, tell me, which one of the three men who saw
> the wounded man proved to be the true neighbor?" The
> religious scholar responded, "The one who demonstrated
> kindness and mercy." Jesus said, "You must go and do
> the same as he."* Luke 10:36-37.

How We Respond To Our Enemies

The Church wants to defeat its enemies; members of the
Body of Christ convert enemies to friends.

> *If your enemy is hungry, buy him lunch! Win him
> over with kindness. For your surprising generosity will
> awaken his conscience, and God will reward you with
> favor. Never let evil defeat you, but defeat evil with good.*
> Romans 12:20-21.

How We Exercise Our Influence

The Church urges support for candidates who will appoint
"the right judges," members of the Body of Christ are
ambassadors who carry His message to the world.

We are ambassadors of the Anointed One who carry the message of Christ to the world, as though God were tenderly pleading with them directly through our lips. So, we tenderly plead with you on Christ's behalf, "Turn back to God and be reconciled to him." 2 Corinthians 5:20.

How We Demonstrate Our Faith

The Church defends itself against attacks on its faith; members of the Body of Christ practice their faith through serving others.

For we remember before our God and Father how you put your faith into practice, how your love motivates you to serve others, and how unrelenting is your hope-filled patience in our Lord Jesus Christ. I Thessalonians 1:3.

What We Are Trying To Change

The Church advocates for political change; members of the Body of Christ seek to change the hearts of individuals toward God.

However, some of the believers from Cyprus and Cyrene, who had come to Antioch in Syria, preached to the non-Jews living there, proclaiming the message of salvation in the Lord Jesus. The mighty power of the Lord was with them as they ministered, and a large number of people believed and turned their hearts to the Lord. Acts 11:20-21.

How We Try To Bring About Change

The Church exercises power to advance righteous causes; members of the Body of Christ do "commendable things" so that others will give their praise to God.

> *"Your lives light up the world. Let others see your light from a distance … Let it shine brightly before others, so that the commendable things you do will shine as light upon them, and then they will give their praise to your Father in heaven."* Matthew 5:14-16.

When we understand the differences between The Church and the Body of Christ and adopt a mindset that reflects our membership in *His* Church, we can more effectively engage in Church reformation.

WHAT WE MEAN BY REFORMATION

My working definition of church reformation, inspired by Alan Caron, is changing the ways and practices of the Church while strengthening its fundamental values and principles.[120] This definition is not meant to *change* the calling of the Church to disciple nations. Quite the contrary, our desire is to strengthen the fundamentals of the Church so that it becomes influential enough to *fulfill* its calling.

In his "Letter From Birmingham Jail"[121], Dr. King discussed the nature of the Church's influence by describing the actions of "early Christians:"

---

120 See, Appendix for a definition of "values" and a definition of "principles."

121 See, African Studies Center, University of Pennsylvania: retrieved from https://www.africa.upenn.edu/Articles_Gen/Letter_Birmingham.html

"There was a time when the church was very powerful. During that period, the early Christians rejoiced when they were deemed worthy to suffer for what they believed. In those days, the church was not merely a thermometer that recorded the ideas and principles of popular opinion; it was the thermostat that transformed the mores of society. Wherever the early Christians entered a town the power structure got disturbed and immediately sought to convict them for being 'disturbers of the peace' and 'outside agitators.' But they went on with the conviction that they were 'a colony of heaven' and had to obey God rather than man. They were small in number but big in commitment. They were too God-intoxicated to be 'astronomically intimidated.' They brought an end to such ancient evils as infanticide and gladiatorial contest."

As highlighted by this excerpt, Church reformation is not just about change; it is about influencing society at large. One way to discuss the Church's influence is to adopt Dr. King's comparison of the Church to a thermostat.

The Body of Christ has always been called to be a thermostat, changing the world to reflect Kingdom values and principles.[122] To take but one example, Jesus turned the leadership model on its head by emphasizing one of our most important Kingdom principles, service motivated by love:

Jesus, knowing their thoughts, called them to his side and said, "Kings and those with great authority in this

---

122 *You see, every child of God overcomes the world, for our faith is the victorious power that triumphs over the world.* I John 5:4

*world rule oppressively over their subjects, like tyrants.
But this is not your calling. You will lead by a completely
different model. The greatest one among you will live as
the one who is called to serve others because* the greatest
honor and authority is reserved for the one with
the heart of a servant. *For even the Son of Man did
not come expecting to be served by everyone, but to serve
everyone, and to give his life in exchange for the salvation
of many."* Matthew 20:25-28.

Unfortunately, it is too often the case that the Church in
America is not a thermostat but a thermometer, one that
reflects the thoughts and behaviors of society at large. For
example, one national Christian commentator noted that
the "political landscape [is] dominated by polarization,
hostility, and misunderstanding."[123] Yet, he noted, some
Christians are not changing the landscape; instead, they
"shout one another down, bully those who disagree, or
exclude one another and refuse to listen."[124]

Thus, it bears repeating, reformation is not just about
changing the Church's ways and practices; it is also about
strengthening its values and principles. Accomplishing both
is critical if the Church is ever going to act as a thermostat,
one that transforms America into a sheep nation that obeys
all Jesus has commanded His disciples.[125]

---

123 See, Timothy Dalrymple, "The Flag in the Whirlwind: An Update from CT's President," *Christianity
Today*, December 22, 2019, accessed from https://www.christianitytoday.com/ct/2019/december-
web-only/trump-evangelicals-editorial-christianity-today-president.html

124 Ibid

125 See, Matthew 25:31-40 and Matthew 28:18-20

THE HEART OF REFORMATION: CHANGING OUR WAYS AND PRACTICES

Now that we have a better idea of what we mean by "Church" and what we mean by "reformation," we can now turn to some thoughts about how we can bring Church reformation in America to pass.

Reformation begins with being inwardly transformed by the Holy Spirit through a total reformation of how we think.[126] This includes a greater appreciation of our role as members of the Body of Christ. We must also cease our imitation of the ideals and opinions of the culture around us.[127] By embracing a new mindset and relinquishing our hold on the culture, we can more easily change our ways and practices.

Set forth below, in summary form, are seven changes the members of the Body of Christ can make that help us display our values and principles to an even greater extent.

FROM	TO
Taking An Institutional View	**Taking A Relational View**

[from valuing *what* we are to valuing *who* we are]

Every believer was faithfully devoted to following the teachings of the apostles. Their hearts were mutually linked to one another, sharing communion and coming together regularly for prayer. … All the believers were in fellowship as one body, and they shared with one another

---

126 See, Romans 12:2

127 Ibid

whatever they had. ... Daily they met together in the temple courts and in one another's homes to celebrate communion. They shared meals together with joyful hearts and tender humility. They were continually filled with praises to God, enjoying the favor of all the people. Acts 2:42-47.

Reacting To People   Responding to Holy Spirit
[from listening to what "they" say to hearing the Holy Spirit]

"Demonstrate love to your neighbor, even as you care for and love yourself." But if you continue to criticize and come against each other over minor issues, you're acting like wild beasts trying to destroy one another! As you yield freely and fully to the dynamic life and power of the Holy Spirit, you will abandon the cravings of your self— life. Galatians 5:14-16

Fighting Culture Wars   Establishing God's Kingdom
[from trying to convince others about our positions to bringing
the Kingdom of Heaven to earth]

Be committed to teach the believers all these things when you are with them in the presence of the Lord. Instruct them to never be drawn into meaningless arguments, or tear each other down with useless words that only harm others. Always be eager to present yourself before God as a perfect and mature minister, without shame, as one who correctly explains the Word of Truth. And avoid empty chatter and worthless words, for they simply add to the irreverence of those who converse in that manner. 2 Timothy 2:14-16.

Defending Our Rights   Advancing God's Kingdom

[from protecting constitutional rights to advancing Kingdom righteousness]

"So above all, constantly chase after the realm of God's kingdom and the righteousness that proceeds from him. Matthew 6:33.

Holding The Right Beliefs   Taking The Right Actions

[from placing importance on political positions
to loving God and our neighbors]

Your calling is to fulfill the royal law of love as given to us in this Scripture: "You must love and value your neighbor as you love and value yourself!" For keeping this law is the noble way to live. But when you show prejudice you commit sin and you violate this royal law of love! James 2:8-9.

Achieving Ends   Respecting / Honoring Others

[from focusing on the "right" results to engaging in the "right" actions.]

Remind people to respect their governmental leaders on every level as law-abiding citizens and to be ready to fulfill their civic duty. And remind them to never tear down anyone with their words or quarrel, but instead be considerate, humble, and courteous to everyone. Titus 3:1-3.

Forcing Compliance   Changing Hearts

[from prohibiting the conduct of others to helping
others encounter a good Father]

Finally, as members of God's beloved family, we must go after the one who wanders from the truth and bring him

*back. For the one who restores the sinning believer back
to God from the error of his way, gives back to his soul
life from the dead, and covers over countless sins by their
demonstration of love!* James 5:19-20.

Each of these shifts advances values or principles that
reflect our love of God, our love of His righteousness, and
our love of His people. Each shift brings the Church closer
to a change in how it accomplishes its goals (e.g., through
members of the Body of Christ). Each shift brings it closer
to a change in how it performs its regular activities (e.g.,
commendable acts performed by ambassadors of Christ).

The Result of Reformation

The reformation of the American Church involves changes
to the Church's ways and practices. These changes
must make an impact outside of the Church if Christ's
ambassadors are going to fulfill our call to disciple the
United States. One way to make such an impact is by
adopting ways and practices that impact how we live our
daily lives.

To leverage that impact, we must demonstrate our values
as well as proclaim our values. Faith that does not involve
action is phony.[128] And love that is not shared through our
deeds is just an abstract theory.[129]

So, what are the tangible actions the Church can take as
a result of focusing even more intently on:

---

128 James 2:17
129 I John 3:18

✤ Taking a relational view,

✤ Responding to the Holy Spirit,

✤ Establishing God's Kingdom,

✤ Advancing God's Kingdom,

✤ Taking The Right Actions,

✤ Respecting & Honoring Others, and

✤ Changing Hearts.

One way to illustrate the nature of those actions is to highlight the difference between the Church as a thermometer and the Church as a thermostat. Set forth below are thought starters/examples of actions we can take to positively change our marriages, families, workplaces, schools, business dealings, communities, and civic participation. The Appendix contains a more detailed list of thought starters.

Marriage and Family

Thermometer: The divorce rate among Christians is not much different from the divorce rate among non-Christians. Moreover, "children from Christian families are about twice as likely as non-Christian children to reside in single-parent households."[130]

Thermostat: Some churches offer pre-marital, marital, and family counseling services to their members. What if even more churches offer such services to their community regardless of church or religious affiliation?

---

130 Michael Gryboski, "U.S. children, Christian children more likely to be raised in single-parent homes: Pew," *The Christian Post*, December 19, 2019, access https://www.christianpost.com/news/us-children-christian-children-more-likely-to-be-raised-in-single-parent-homes-pew.html

Workplace

Thermometer: Christians tend to adopt the behaviors in their workplace environment.[131]

Thermostat: Some Christians start Bible studies in their workplaces. What if even more Christians started common interest groups and mentoring programs based on Kingdom principles and opened membership to their co-workers regardless of affiliation?

Public Schools

Thermometer: Christians are just as likely as non-Christians to criticize public schools, but our response is not to change the "climate" of public schools but to leave public schools.[132]

Thermostat: What if even more local churches partnered with local schools to pray for school administrators and faculty and to help start programs that enrich all students; what if even more local churches operated after-school/ homework/recreation programs for all neighborhood children, regardless of affiliation?

The Community

Thermometer: Often, a homeowner drives into their garage at night and drives out of their garage in the

---

131 See, Michael Gryboski, "Former Trump admin insider talks 2020 election, challenges to his Christian faith," *Christian Post,* February 18, 2019, accessed https://www.christianpost.com/news/former-trump-admin-insider-talks-2020-election-challenges-to-his-christian-faith.html

132 See, David d'Escoto, "10 Big Reasons Not to Send Christian Kids to Public Schools," *Crosswalk.com,* April 10, 2012 accessed https://www.crosswalk.com/family/homeschool/10-big-reasons-not-to-send-christian-kids-to-public-schools-11603305.html

morning without any interaction with their neighbors. Similarly, some church members drive into their church's neighborhood on a Sunday and drive out a few hours later without any interaction with the neighbors.

Thermostat: What if even more local churches partnered with others in the community, regardless of affiliation, to identify needs in the community and empathetically came alongside the people in the community to meet that need?

Business / Economics:

Thermometer: Christians are guided by "business" or "professional" ethics (even when those ethics are contrary or inconsistent with Kingdom values).

Thermostat: What if even more Christians introduced and supported business practices and economic methodologies that increase the presence of Kingdom values (e.g., the economics of mutuality)?

Government / Politics

Thermometer: Christians pursue Kingdom outcomes but behave like other candidates and incumbents and their supporters, e.g., engaging in or tolerating negative campaigning.

Thermostat: What if even more Christians focused on reducing divisiveness and partisanship in political and civil discourse by devoting themselves to loving others, respecting and honoring them regardless of affiliation?

Even as we demonstrate Christlike love in tangible ways, we must never forget that reconciling sons and daughters with their Heavenly Father is at the heart of everything we do.[133] Even as we increase the presence of Kingdom values in our culture, we must remember that we are Christ's ambassadors. Our ministry is to tenderly plead with others through our words and actions on the Messiah's behalf, "Turn back to God and be reconciled to Him."

SUMMARY

Reformation of the Church is defined as a change in ways and practices that help *The* Church strengthen its identity as *His* Church, the Body of Christ.

Reformation of the Church begins when we "stop imitating the ideals and opinions of the culture around us," and we display our fundamental values and principles to an even greater extent.

Reformation is enabled when we realize that we are many members of one body, the Body of Christ, His Church.

Reformation of the Church transforms society when its ways and practices shift society from one climate, where we will *"find many troubles and every kind of meanness,"* to another climate *"filled with love"* James 3:16-18.

---

133 2 Corinthians 5:17-21 (see the appendix for the full quote)

FINAL WORDS: RADICAL REFORMERS

His Church must not only be radically reformed, but it must also lead to radical reformation. In today's society, it is radical to lead by serving[134] and to love by doing,[135] but Jesus changed the world by being a radical who did the radical.[136] His Church must be and do likewise.

Shalom!

APPENDIX

Thought Starters

The following is a list of thought-starters for what the Church can do to change the climate in its spheres of influence. Some of them reflect a key attribute of a thermostat in that they affect the entire environment, not just the Christian environment.

Marriage and Family

Thermometer: The divorce rate among Christians is not much different from the divorce rate among non-Christians. Moreover, "children from Christian families are about twice

---

134 *the greatest one among you will live as the one who is called to serve others.* Matthew 20:26;

135 *our love can't be an abstract theory we only talk about, but a way of life demonstrated through our loving deeds.* I John 3:18

136 *For even the Son of Man did not come expecting to be served by everyone, but to serve everyone, and to give his life in exchange for the salvation of many.* Matthew 20:28.

as likely as non-Christian children to reside in single-parent households."[137]

Thermostat: Perhaps the Church can *reduce the overall number and adverse effects of divorces and unwanted single-parent households* in America by:

✤ offering programs that sustain marriage and strengthen the family (e.g., pre-marital counseling; marriage and family counseling, etc.) to people regardless of religious affiliation;

✤ embracing single-parent households in the community of believers and being intentional about implementing programs tailored for them;

✤ taking a leadership role in our communities in facilitating and encouraging families, regardless of religious or church affiliation, to adopt children through Kingdom-minded adoption agencies;

✤ sponsoring and encouraging mature men and women to participate in or form mentoring, e.g., big brother—big sister programs.

Workplace

Thermometer: Christians tend to adopt the behaviors in their workplace environment.[138]

Thermostat: Perhaps Christians can influence employees to adopt Kingdom behaviors by, to an even greater extent;

---

137 Michael Gryboski, "U.S. children, Christian children more likely to be raised in single-parent homes: Pew," *The Christian Post*, December 19, 2019, access https://www.christianpost.com/news/us-children-christian-children-more-likely-to-be-raised-in-single-parent-homes-pew.html

138 See, Michael Gryboski, "Former Trump admin insider talks 2020 election, challenges to his Christian faith," *Christian Post*, February 18, 2019, accessed https://www.christianpost.com/news/former-trump-admin-insider-talks-2020-election-challenges-to-his-christian-faith.html

❖ coming in the opposite spirit, e.g., responding to undermining with respect and honor;

❖ leading by serving;

❖ loving people who regard us as an enemy, blessing those who curse us, doing something wonderful for those who hate us;

❖ starting Bible studies, prayer groups;

❖ starting common interest groups for employees regardless of religious affiliation; and

❖ starting mentoring programs for people regardless of religious affiliation.

Public Schools

Thermometer: Christians are just as likely as non-Christians to criticize public schools, but our response is not to change the "climate" of public schools but to leave public schools.[139]

Thermostat: Perhaps the Church can *increase the presence of Kingdom values in public schools* when, to an even greater extent,

❖ Christian parents spend time not only teaching our children values but also teaching our children how to share their values with others at their schools;

❖ Christian parents and local churches teach and equip children how to form Bible studies and prayer groups in public schools;

---

139 See, David d'Escoto, "10 Big Reasons Not to Send Christian Kids to Public Schools," *Crosswalk.com,* April 10, 2012 accessed https://www.crosswalk.com/family/homeschool/10-big-reasons-not-to-send-christian-kids-to-public-schools-11603305.html

❖ Christian parents are even more involved in school administration, including school boards;

❖ local churches partner with local schools to pray for school administrators and faculty and participate in programs that enrich all students, and

❖ local churches operate after-school/homework/recreation programs for all neighborhood children, regardless of religious affiliation.

The Community

Thermometer: Often, a homeowner drives into their garage at night and drives out of their garage in the morning without any interaction with their neighbors. Similarly, some church members drive into their church's neighborhood on a Sunday and drive out a few hours later without any interaction with the neighbors.

Thermostat: Perhaps the Church can *increase the mutual concern that neighbors in a community have for one another* when its members, to an even greater extent,

❖ participate in the community as a good neighbor (as opposed to as the local preacher);

❖ identify needs in the community and empathetically come alongside the people in the community to meet that need, and

❖ participate with other community members in acts of service, e.g., launching and operating a community center, motivated by love.

Business / Economics:

Thermometer: Christians adhere to "business" or "professional" ethics (even when those ethics are contrary or inconsistent with Kingdom values).

Thermostat: Perhaps the Church *can increase the presence of Kingdom values in the marketplace* when it, to an even greater extent,

❖ introduces and supports business practices and economic methodologies that increase the presence of Kingdom values (e.g., the economics of mutuality);

❖ practices honest dealing even when less than honest dealing is a standard business practice, e.g., buyer beware (don't ask to don't tell re: product deficiencies);

❖ launches businesses that meet community needs and employs people from the neighborhood in those businesses; and

❖ engages in social entrepreneurship.

Government / Politics

Thermometer: The Church pursues Kingdom outcomes but behaves like other candidates and incumbents and their supporters, e.g., engaging in or tolerating negative campaigning.

Thermostat: Perhaps the Church can *reduce the amount of divisiveness and partisanship in political and civil discourse* when its members, to an even greater extent,

❖ support candidates for political office who display the attributes of an ambassador for Christ,

❖ display the fruit of the Spirit as they engage in campaigning,

❖ outdo others in showing respect and honor to others,

❖ love people who regard them as enemies, bless those who curse them, do something wonderful for the one who hates them and pray for those who persecute them.

Definitions

Values

"Values are basic and fundamental beliefs that guide or motivate attitudes or actions. They help us to determine what is important to us … They provide the general guidelines for conduct."[140]

Principles

A fundamental truth or proposition that serves as the foundation for a system of belief or behavior.[141]

A general belief about the way you should behave, which influences your behavior.[142]

Scriptures

I Corinthians 12:12-14

Just as the human body is one, though it has many parts that together form one body, so too is Christ. For by one Spirit we

---

140 Ethics Sage, retrieved from https://www.ethicssage.com/2018/08/what-are-values.html

141 Lexico, retrieved from https://www.lexico.com/en/definition/principle

142 Collins Dictionary, retrieved from https://www.collinsdictionary.com/us/dictionary/english/principle

all were immersed and mingled into one single body. And no matter our status—whether we are Jews or non-Jews, oppressed or free—we are all privileged to drink deeply of the same Holy Spirit. In fact, the human body is not one single part but rather many parts mingled into one.

Romans 12:4-5

In the human body there are many parts and organs, each with a unique function. And so it is in the body of Christ. For though we are many, we've all been mingled into one body in Christ. This means that we are all vitally joined to one another, with each contributing to the others.

Ephesians 4:15-16

But instead we will remain strong and always sincere in our love as we express the truth. All our direction and ministries will flow from Christ and lead us deeper into him, the anointed Head of his body, the church. For his "body" has been formed in his image and is closely joined together and constantly connected as one. And every member has been given divine gifts to contribute to the growth of all; and as these gifts operate effectively throughout the whole body, we are built up and made perfect in love.

Isaiah 1:10-19

Hear the word of the Lord, You rulers of Sodom; Give ear to the law of our God, You people of Gomorrah: "To what purpose is the multitude of your sacrifices to Me?" Says the Lord. "I have had enough of burnt offerings of rams And the fat of fed cattle. I do not delight in the blood of bulls, Or of lambs or goats. "When you come to appear before Me, Who has required this from your hand, To trample My courts? Bring no more futile sacrifices; Incense is an abomination to Me. The New Moons, the Sabbaths, and the calling of assemblies—I cannot endure iniquity and the sacred meeting. Your New Moons and your appointed feasts My soul hates; They are a trouble to Me, I am weary of bearing them. When you spread out your hands, I will hide My eyes from you; Even though you make many prayers, I will not hear. Your hands are full of blood. "Wash yourselves, make yourselves clean; Put away the evil of your doings from before My eyes. Cease to do evil, Learn to do good; Seek justice, Rebuke the oppressor; Defend the fatherless, Plead for the widow. "Come now, and let us reason together," Says the Lord, "Though your sins are like scarlet, They shall be as white as snow; Though they are red like crimson, They shall be as wool. If you are willing and obedient, You shall eat the good of the land;

Isaiah 58:3-7

Why have we fasted,' they say, 'and You have not seen? Why have we afflicted our souls, and You take no notice?' "In fact, in the day of your fast you find pleasure, And exploit all your laborers. Indeed you fast for strife and debate, And to strike with the fist of wickedness. You will not fast as you do this day, To make your voice heard on high. Is it a fast that I have chosen, A day for a man to afflict his soul? Is it to bow down his head like a bulrush, And to spread out sackcloth and ashes? Would you call this a fast, And an acceptable day to the Lord?"Is this not the fast that I have chosen: To loose the bonds of wickedness, To undo the heavy burdens, To let the oppressed go free, And that you break every yoke? Is it not to share your bread with the hungry, And that you bring to your house the poor who are cast out; When you see the naked, that you cover him, And not hide yourself from your own flesh?

2 Corinthians 5:17-21

*Now, if anyone is enfolded into Christ, he has become an entirely
new creation. All that is related to the old order has vanished.
Behold, everything is fresh and new. And God has made all
things new, and reconciled us to himself, and given us the
ministry of reconciling others to God. In other words, it was
through the Anointed One that God was shepherding the world,
not even keeping records of their transgressions, and he has
entrusted to us the ministry of opening the door of reconciliation
to God. We are ambassadors of the Anointed One who carry the
message of Christ to the world, as though God were tenderly
pleading with them directly through our lips. So we tenderly
plead with you on Christ's behalf, "Turn back to God and be
reconciled to him." For God made the only one who did not
know sin to become sin for us, so that we who did not know
righteousness might become the righteousness of God through
our union with him.*

Chapter Seven
Church In The Community

"What goes on inside our four walls, inside the church building, should happen all over the city." — Dr. Ed Silvoso.[143]

In his book, *The Church in the Workplace,* Dr. C. Peter Wagner describes the "faith at work" movement. According to Dr. Wagner, this movement seriously escalated in the 1990s when "many of the authors on the subject began to gain the understanding that what believers do in the workplace is a legitimate form of Christian ministry."[144] This "movement" became known as Church in the Workplace or Church in the Marketplace.

As Dr. Wagner noted: "the true church of Jesus Christ … does not only take the form of … congregations of believers that meet together for worship on Sundays … [it] also takes the form of dispersion of believers out in the workplace the other six days of the week."[145]

Church in the Marketplace is not about holding church services in our workplaces. It is about engaging in ministry or acts of service in our workplaces.

---

143 Rachel Phua, "Your workplace, your harvest field,: *Salt & Light,* June 29, 2018 accessed, https://saltandlight.sg/work/your-workplace-the-harvest-field/

144 C. Peter Wagner, *The Church in the Workplace,* (Regal Books. Ventura CA 2006), 82

145 Wagner, *The Church in the Workplace,* 6

But if the goal is, as Dr. Wagner stated, to "bring us to the place where we will be doing our part to glorify God through the actual transformation of society itself,"[146] we must extend the Church beyond the four walls of the workplace as well as the four walls of the sanctuary.

If we are to transform society, the Church must engage in ministry in our communities.

In his book, *On Earth as it is in Heaven*, Dr. Wagner recounts a comment by John Maxwell: "One of my major mistakes was thinking that life revolved around the local church and what we were doing. For example, if you were a member of a church, you had to have a ministry in the church." He goes on to say, "I had a lot of high-capacity people who were probably never 'salt and light' like they could have been. I would change that immediately if I went back to the local church. I would be a lot more into how we influenced our community than how I could get everybody on board with my church program."[147]

As Jack Graham of Prestonwood Baptist Church in Dallas, Texas, said: "Revival will come when we get the walls down between the Church and the community." (Wagner, 2011).

All of us are members of a community regardless of where we worship and regardless of where we work or whether we work. "To be a disciple of Jesus means you are part of a community by definition."

---

146 Ibid

147 C. Peter Wagner, *On Earth As It Is In Heaven: Answer God's Call To Transform The World* (Regal Books, Ventura, CA 2012), 38

Even if I serve at church, even if I minister at work, I am also a member of the community in which I live. Loving and serving my neighbors is another way I can contribute to the transformation of society.

There are plenty of opportunities to minister in both the marketplace and the community but they are different. Let's compare the two settings.

MARKETPLACE	COMMUNITY
Hierarchical / vertical view of interactions	Relational / horizontal view
Populated by bosses and employees	Populated by friends and neighbors
Families not included	Families an integral part
Nine to Five	Any time
Monday—Friday	Any day
Marketplace is made up of organizations	Community is made up of people

The two settings are not mutually exclusive. In fact, the marketplace and the community overlap. Most businesses are small businesses, and they are vital parts of the community.

However, there are meaningful differences between the two. We can see those differences in the basic definition of the words.

The Oxford Dictionary defines "marketplace" as the arena of commercial dealings.[148] This same dictionary defines "community" as a group of people living in the same place or having a particular characteristic in common.[149]

Briefly stated, the marketplace is where I conduct business. The community is where I live.

Think about what happens in the local shopping center. When we see it as the hub of commercial activity (I can shop for groceries at one store, find something to eat at restaurants, get my hair cut or my nails done, get my clothes dry cleaned, fill a prescription, buy a lamp) it is a place for me to conduct business.

If I see that same local shopping center as part of the community, then the people who work in the shopping center are not just service providers; they are neighbors. Over time as relationships develop, they become individual people. My dry cleaner and my barber know me by name and know that I am involved in ministry. I converse with some of my neighbors more often in the local grocery store than in my home or theirs (sadly).

To leverage this difference into expanded opportunities to minister requires a shift in our mindset.

Before Church in the Marketplace, the workplace was where I worked. After Church in the Marketplace, the workplace was also where I could minister.

---

148 Oxford Living Dictionaries (2017). Oxford, United Kingdom: Oxford University Press accessed October 1, 2018 https://en.oxforddictionaries.com/definition/marketplace

149 Oxford Living Dictionaries (2017). Oxford, United Kingdom: Oxford University Press accessed October 1, 2018 https://en.oxforddictionaries.com/definition/community

Similarly, we must understand the community is not just where I live. The community is also where I can minister.

What are the implications for how we act when our mindset has been expanded to include Church in the Community?

We are members of a community regardless of where we worship and regardless of where we work or whether we work. "To be a disciple of Jesus means you are part of a community by definition."[150]

Even if I serve at church, even if I minister at work, I am also a member of the community in which I live. Loving and serving my neighbors is another way I can contribute to the transformation of society.

Set forth below are some of the differences between a marketplace mindset and a community mindset.

MARKETPLACE	COMMUNITY
I influence the workplace	I influence the community
Goal: success	Goal: service
My labor is ministry	Loving my neighbor is ministry
What I do counts	Who I am counts

Recognizing that we are part of a community expands the focus from individual people in the workplace

---

150 Doug Greenwold, "Two Very Different Worlds: Western Evangelicalism and the Gospels," *Preserving Bible Times*, accessed May 14, 2018 http://preservingbibletimes.org/wp-content/uploads/2014/03/Reflection.TwoWorlds1.pdf

influencing *their* environment to people in the community engaging in collective action to change *the* environment.

But engaging in collective action requires us to let go of our separate and solitary pursuits to change *our* world (the result of a Western mindset of rugged individualism) and embrace collective actions that can change *the* world. However, that's an essay for another time.

Part Three:

Loving Our Enemies

During His Sermon on the Mount, Jesus asks: *What reward do you deserve if you only love the loveable? Don't even the tax collectors do that? How are you any different from others if you limit your kindness only to your friends? Don't even the ungodly do that?* Matthew 5:46-47.

God so loved the world that He gave His only Son as a sacrifice so that all who believed in Him would have eternal life. Jesus' questions remind us that the God kind of love is not reserved for our friends. It is to be demonstrated to everyone, even the unlovable.

The essays in Part Three reflect my own struggles to love those who regard me as an enemy, bless the one who curses me, do something wonderful for the one who hates me, and pray for the very ones who persecute me by praying for them.

Once I saw myself as God saw me, and once I loved the Church as God loved it, my struggles were over. The primary goal of Part Three is to help us overcome some of the obstacles that make it difficult to love people who may regard us as enemies.

Chapter 8: I Have Met The Enemy, And He Is Me: It is
said that silence is complicity. Can you be complicit in
your own oppression? This essay discusses some of the
uncomfortable situations I faced in predominantly white
evangelical environments. It explores my complicity in
allowing those situations to continue. And it ends with
a life-changing revelation from a loving God.

*Chapter 9: I'm the Good Samaritan? Even Those Who Regard Me
As An Enemy Are My Neighbors.* I acknowledge my feelings
about church leaders who used the Bible to justify slavery,
Jim Crow, and racial inequality in this essay. But those
feelings aren't as strong as my love for the Church. Like
the man encountered by the Good Samaritan, the Church is
hurting. I can't just cross the street and walk on by.

Chapter Eight

I Have Met The Enemy, And He Is Me

"I am an invisible man. No, I am not a spook like those who haunted Edgar Allen Poe: Nor am I one of your Hollywood movie ectoplasms. I am a man of substance, flesh and bone, fiber and liquids, and I might even be said to possess a mind. I am invisible, simply because people refuse to see me."[151]

As an African American who was part of primarily white evangelical environments for many years, these comments from the main character in the novel, *Invisible Man*, resonate with me. Too often, people in those environments saw my skin color, but they refused to see *me*.

I don't mean to imply that anyone mistreated me. But as the character in the novel says, "I felt that even when they were polite, they hardly saw *me*" (emphasis added). Although there were times when this made me uncomfortable, I lived with it.

After the deaths of Armaud Arbery, George Floyd, and Breonna Taylor, my own emotions and well-meaning

---

151 Ralph Ellison, *Invisible Man*, (Random House. NY, NY 1980)

friends forced me to examine my history in these
environments. In doing so, I was stunned by the extent
to which I had excused behavior, overlooked slights, and
given passes to well-meaning people.

I had buried all of it in a shallow grave. Then one day,
a rallying cry of those seeking racial justice, "silence is
complicity," rang loudly in my ears.

I had been silent. I was complicit in how I allowed others
to treat me.

But why?

Why had I been silent about my negative experiences
in primarily white evangelical environments? Was it my
people-pleasing nature? Was I afraid of confrontation? Was
I placing a higher value on peace? Maybe it was enough for
me that the vast majority of my interactions were positive.

These reasons, to the extent they were ever true, no longer
justified my silence.

To end my silence, I scheduled a meeting with my former
boss and former pastor. At the time of the meeting, I had
returned to the fold as his network's executive director.

The pastor was a friend. He was one of my spiritual
mentors. He had commissioned me as an apostle. And he
was also an unwitting contributor to some of my most
uncomfortable experiences.

But by the time of our meeting, I realized I had been
complicit in my own discomfort.

Before my meeting, I captured my thoughts on paper.
I wanted to mitigate the possibility of being an incoherent
mess during the meeting. What follows is an edited version
of what I wrote (I have changed the names to ensure that
the intent of sharing my thoughts, my complicity, remains
the focus, not the people involved):

*There is racial insensitivity in the "church" family. There.
I said it.*

*I have contributed to the existence of racial insensitivity in the
"church" family. There. I said it.*

I am part of the problem.

*I have valued peace in the family more than my discomfort.
I have valued my reputation more than affirmative change. I have
valued "Pastor's" heart more than the [uncomfortable] truth.*

*If I did not value peace so much, I would have shared with
Pastor that there are times I feel invisible in some church
settings, including my own church. I would have found a way
to let Pastor know how often I get the once over, the twice
over, the thrice over at church events because I am the only
African American in the green room; that other attendees have
asked conference hosts to question me about my presence in
the reserved section.*

*I would have shared that there are times when I feel invisible
in my own "house," my church's sanctuary; that there are
conference speakers who have never given me eye contact
during their multiple appearances at our conferences; and that
some of them studiously avoid eye contact when they pass me
in the hallways.*

If I did not value my reputation so much (by avoiding the label of self-promoter), I would have asked to be more visible in the apostolic network. My mom, who taught me not to call attention to myself, would be proud of the fact that I didn't seek to leverage my leadership role to be more visible; but failing to be more insistent about the value of African Americans seeing people who look like them in positions of influence did not serve the network well.

If I did not value my knowledge of the sincerity of Pastor's heart so much, I would have shared with him the silent signal he unknowingly sends to white leaders in his circle when he does not introduce me to them; that when he does not introduce me, he unknowingly gives people permission to treat me as invisible or less than. He gives them permission to treat me with suspicion ("What's he doing here?")

But I, too, have been silent. I have been complicit. Lord, please forgive me for what my silence has wrought in Your house. Pastor, please forgive me for not sharing my experiences. Please forgive me for not giving you an opportunity to do what I know is in your heart to do, which is the God-honoring thing.

And, by and large, this is what I shared with Pastor.[152] I apologized for not giving him an opportunity to act on my behalf. If I had any doubts that he would have done so had I asked, he dispelled them a few weeks later.

During a group Zoom call with leaders in the network, I broke my silence to ask him how to raise racial equality issues without seeming self-serving. He teared up as

---

152 With all due respect to how loving and kind the Pastor was during the conversation, I am sharing my notes rather than the conversation to retain the focus on my complicity.

he told the group I was one of the most unselfish and generous persons he knew.

To be sure, our meeting was uncomfortable. Pastor was clearly empathetic. He took the time to understand better what I was saying and feeling. But beyond that, given the passage of time, neither one of us was quite sure what to do next.

Shortly after that, I was asked to write, from my perspective as an African American, a column in the network's newsletter about the "racial unrest" that was taking place after the death of George Floyd.

However, in my then role as the network's executive director, I was also asked to write an article about the tangible things we could do as a network to combat systematic racism.

Maybe I was visible after all.

In the column, I wrote:

I'm sure most of us in [the network] are outraged by systematic racism in our society. But what will we do about it?

Part of the answer is to seek racial justice through Spirit-led unity.

> The Lord has formed His body "intentionally" so that every member would look after the others with mutual concern, and so that there will be no division in the body. In that way, whatever happens to one member happens to all. "If one suffers, everyone suffers. If one is honored, everyone rejoices," I Corinthians 12:25-26.

It starts with us. We must look after one another in [the network] with mutual concern; whatever happens to one member, e.g., racism, happens to all. **We must be united as one body.**

We serve a God of love, thus, the key to unity is to love each other unconditionally. **But we must put that love into action.** *As we do so, we will be guided by three principles.*

We will be activists in the pursuit of unity; our activism will be Spirit-led;

We will contend for unity by contending against that which contends against unity;

We will value every member of the Body.

We will actively recruit people of color to become members; people of color will be valued participants at all levels of [the network], from speaking engagements to decision-making; we will not support legislative (and other) positions in a way that devalues the lives of people of color.

We urge every member and their networks to adopt behaviors and take actions in their communities in alignment with these principles. (emphasis in the original).

In the months after the newsletter was published, the network increased its focus on issues such as religious liberty and pro-life political advocacy. It advocated that all lives are sacred. To my knowledge, no member of the network adopted the guiding principles in my article.

Me?

I became invisible again.

I no longer frequent the same primarily white evangelical environments I was such a part of for so many years. Nor do I avoid them.

As I continued to wrestle with my invisibility, I was invited to teach in a different, primarily white evangelical environment in a city known for its racism (it was once the state headquarters for the KKK). In a wonderful, only God set of circumstances, my wife and I experienced much more than politeness.

We have been claimed as spiritual mentors and friends by the senior pastors. We have been embraced by their church family, a primarily white evangelical environment. We live 1400 miles from them.

But we are visible. People see *us*.

As I shared with the senior pastors, I am still in awe that they asked me to be their spiritual mentor. And I am still in awe at how strong I desire to be even more connected to them, their spiritual family, and to what they are doing to transform their city.

More importantly, I am in awe of God. He has destroyed the lie that I was invisible or that I ever could be.

Chapter Nine

I'm The Good Samaritan?!: Even Those Who Regard Me As An Enemy Are My Neighbors

In a scene from the movie *Addams Family Values*, children attending summer camp put on a Thanksgiving play. In the play, the pilgrims have invited their "new primitive friends" to dinner. All seems to go well until one of the "primitive friends" announces, "we cannot break bread with you."

She goes on to outline the differences between "my people" and "your people" ("Years from now my people will be forced to live in mobile homes on reservations. Your people will wear cardigans and drink highballs"). The "primitive friends" then turn the tables on the pilgrims. The "primitive friends" become the hosts and the pilgrims the uncomfortable guests.[153]

The history of humankind is filled with the differences between "my people" and "your people."

By the time of the first Thanksgiving in 1621, "my people"

were already enslaved in America ("For centuries my people will be enslaved and forced to work on land that is not theirs. Your people will explore lands to the west and claim them as their own").

The differences between "my people" and "your people" are a feature of African Americans' history in the American Church. The differences are complicated. Both peoples serve a God for whom such differences make no difference.

For as many of you as were baptized into Christ have put on Christ. There is neither Jew nor Greek, there is neither slave nor free, there is neither male nor female; for you are all one in Christ Jesus. Galatians 3:27-28.

African Americans have long had to make the distinction between Christ and Christ-followers. There is neither slave nor free in Christ, but there is slave and free among Christians:

Take these words from the African American orator, author, and activist, Frederick Douglass. "I love the pure, peaceable, and impartial Christianity of Christ; I, therefore, hate the corrupt, slaveholding, women-whipping, cradle-plundering, partial, and hypocritical Christianity of this land. Indeed, I can see no reason, but the most deceitful one, for calling the religion of this land Christianity. I look upon it as the climax of all misnomers, the boldest of all frauds, and the grossest of all libels."[154]

Sadly, starting with the formation of the colonies, through slavery, Jim Crow, the civil-rights movement, and present day, leaders in the American Church have been vocal about

---

154 Frederick Douglass, "Narrative of the Life of Frederick Douglass", *Sparknotes*, accessed https://www.sparknotes.com/lit/narrative/full-text/appendix/

their views of African Americans as "less than." While some Church leaders fought for racial equality during these periods, others have been less than enthusiastic. Dr. Martin Luther King, Jr., sums up the feelings of many African American leaders when he wrote:

"I must honestly reiterate that I have been disappointed with the church. I do not say that as one of those negative critics who can always find something wrong with the church. I say it as a minister of the gospel who loves the church, who was nurtured in its bosom, who has been sustained by its Spiritual blessings, and who will remain true to it as long as the cord of life shall lengthen...

"I have heard numerous religious leaders of the South call upon their worshipers to comply with a desegregation decision because it is the law, but I have longed to hear white ministers say, follow this decree because integration is morally right and the Negro is your brother. In the midst of blatant injustices inflicted upon the Negro, I have watched white churches stand on the sidelines and merely mouth pious irrelevancies and sanctimonious trivialities."[155]

My goal here is not to support the validity of what Mr. Douglass and Dr. King have observed. I'm sure many would disagree with one or more of these men, and perhaps, rightly so. However, these observations do inform my own opinion that today there is a "my people" (African Americans) and a "your people" (the American Church). And sometimes, they are at odds.

---

155 African Studies Center, University of Pennsylvania, accessed https://www.africa.upenn.edu/Articles_ Gen/ Letter_Birmingham.html

But shouldn't I know that such a distinction is not God's intent?

My history suggests I should. I gave my life to Christ nearly forty-five years ago. I have taught hundreds of Bible studies. I have been ordained as a deacon, ordained as a pastor, and commissioned as an apostle. I have been a member of nearly a dozen church or ministry boards. I am the academic dean of a Christian university.

Shouldn't I know that *"there is no distinction between Jew and Greek, for the same Lord over all is rich to all who call upon Him"?* Romans 10:12.

God does not recognize distinctions when it comes to salvation. But He does recognize a distinction between people. Those distinctions don't matter to Him, but He recognizes them nonetheless.

My challenge is that these distinctions do matter to me. I was part of primarily white evangelical environments for decades. In these environments, I learned about and embraced the gospel of the Kingdom and the gospel of salvation. I learned that the will of God was to bring the Kingdom of Heaven to earth now, not in the by and by.

The gospel of the Kingdom is such a life-changing, life-affirming message that my desire was to bring even more African Americans into my primarily white evangelical environments. I overlooked the slights I endured from time to time (see, Chapter Eight). I was an enthusiastic attendee of conferences hosted by white evangelical churches and ministries.

But then came the response by some white evangelicals to the protests of the Ahmaud Arbery and George Floyd murders; their response to false allegations against people of color; their response to the idea that black lives matter.

Social media was filled with hateful comments from people who disavowed their affiliation with church leaders because they supported racial equality. I read comments from people in "my stream" (an affiliation of relationships that are not formal enough to be called a denomination) who dismissed the existence of racial discrimination. People who condescendingly tried to educate their African American friends about what the black lives matter movement was really about. Still, others were willing to actively support leaders who espoused white nationalist views so long as those leaders were anti-abortion.

I went from being an active and enthusiastic member of a predominantly white church environment (just as I had been an active and enthusiastic member of predominantly white neighborhoods, predominantly white schools, and predominantly white athletic teams) to feeling like an outsider.

But another feeling began to creep in, betrayal. Upon reflection, that sense of betrayal was less about the conduct of other people and more about my sense of naivete. This sense of treading lightly so others could feel comfortable around me (see, Chapter Eight) meant nothing to them, less than nothing.

Yes, my white evangelical friends cared about racial justice... just not as much as they cared about (in no particular order)

❖ Opposing abortion

❖ Promoting "traditional" marriage

❖ Opposing LGBTQ rights

❖ "Religious" liberty

❖ "Blue lives"

❖ Confederate monuments

❖ A conservative Supreme Court

At least in my eyes, these friends demonstrated that if
a leader supported these things, they need not support
racial justice. In fact, they could speak out against racial
justice (after all, it's part of the socialist, Marxist agenda) so
long as they opposed abortion.

And my friends were okay with me knowing that racial
justice took a backseat to their other issues. I was Greg, the
you're-not-one-of-them-you're-a-good-Negro, Greg. How
could I be offended?

So, yeah, I began to feel a sense of betrayal that led me to
step out of the primarily white evangelical environments
I was frequenting at the time. "Your people" are
contributing to the inequities being visited upon "my
people." How could I be a part of you?

Then I watched a message preached by Judah Smith on one
of the New Testament's most visible "my people" are different
from "your people" parables. It involves Jews and Samaritans.

As author Alice Camille notes about the history of the
two people groups, "Verbal disputes led to insults, insults
to violence. … By the first century, C.E., the worst thing

you can call a Jew is a Samaritan—which is what Jesus' detractors call Him in John's gospel."[156]

This brings us to the parable of the Good Samaritan. Most of us know the parable and the context. In the Gospel, according to Luke, a lawyer asks Jesus, *"Teacher, what shall I do to inherit eternal life?" He said to him, "What is written in the law? What is your reading of it?" So he answered and said, "'You shall love the Lord your God with all your heart, with all your soul, with all your strength, and with all your mind,' and 'your neighbor as yourself.'" And He said to him, "You have answered rightly; do this, and you will live."* Luke 10:25-28.

But the lawyer wasn't finished, *wanting to justify himself, the lawyer asked Jesus, "And who is my neighbor?" Jesus replied, "There was once a Jewish man traveling from Jerusalem to Jericho when bandits robbed him along the way. They beat him severely, stripped him naked, and left him half dead. Soon, a Jewish priest walking down the same road came upon the wounded man. Seeing him from a distance, the priest crossed to the other side of the road and walked right past him, not turning to help him one bit. Later, a religious man, a Levite, came walking down the same road and likewise crossed to the other side to pass by the wounded man without stopping to help him. Finally, another man, a Samaritan, came upon the bleeding man and was moved with tender compassion for him. He stooped down and gave him first aid, pouring olive oil on his wounds, disinfecting them with wine, and bandaging them to stop the bleeding. Lifting him up, he placed him on his own donkey and brought him to an inn. Then he took him from his donkey and carried him to a room for the night. The*

---

156 Alice Camille, "Why didn't the Jews and Samaritans get along?" *U.S. Catholic*, May 4, 2020, accessed https://uscatholic.org/articles/202005/why-didnt-the-jews-and-samaritans-get-along/

next morning he took his own money from his wallet and gave it to the innkeeper with these words: 'Take care of him until I come back from my journey. If it costs more than this, I will repay you when I return.' So, now, tell me, which one of the three men who saw the wounded man proved to be the true neighbor?" The religious scholar responded, "The one who demonstrated kindness and mercy." Jesus said, "Go and do the same as he." Luke 10:29-37.

Prior to the Judah Smith message, I would have used the parable to justify my sense of betrayal. Were these not Jewish leaders who failed to help a fellow Jew? I would have compared the Jewish man left half dead to African American brothers and sisters in Christ. Despite our condition, Christian pastors and other religious leaders were crossing the road and walking right past us without stopping to help. They were too busy pursuing pro-life issues, protecting religious liberty, and defending the institution of marriage to help a brother out.

After the Judah Smith message, my perspective changed. In Pastor Judah's funny but pointed sermon, he asks, "God, do you really mean you want me to stop and help someone who regards me as an enemy? Even the man's own people aren't stopping to help him."

The answer, of course, is "yes."

In Pastor Judah's telling, neighborliness is not only defined by meeting the need but also by the decision to meet the need regardless of *who is in need.*

What makes us neighbors is not proximity. It is not standing. It is not even relationship. What makes us neighbors is the willingness to love regardless of proximity, or relationship, or standing.

So, what was I to do with this revelation? Was I going to identify with the victim and feed my sense of betrayal? Or was I going to identify with the Samaritan and demonstrate kindness and mercy?

Even with my sense of betrayal, these were not difficult questions. Of course, I was going to follow Jesus' encouragement "to go and do the same."

The American Church is clearly hurt. It is hurt by a culture that has taken the views of a relative few Christians to brand it as homophobic, hypocritical, racist, and even mean-spirited. It is hurt by internal divisiveness. It is hurt by its ongoing attempts to come to terms with its role in some of the most ungodly aspects of American history. And let's be clear, it is hurt by people like me who mistakenly feel like the Church owes them something.

I could observe these hurts, cross the street to pursue my own sense of betrayal, and walk on by. But how could I advocate that unconditional love is the way for the Church to heal our culture (as I do in other essays) and then not be at the forefront of demonstrating that same kind of love to heal the Church?

Lord, help me to be moved with tender compassion for the Church. Help me stoop down and give it first aid, stop the bleeding, and bring it to a place where it can rest and be cared for. May I be willing to do whatever it costs to bring it to a place of wholeness. In Jesus' name, I pray. Amen.

Part Four:
Service Motivated By Christlike Love

To give a well-worn phrase a makeover, we can serve without loving, but we cannot love without serving. Unfortunately, we encounter too many examples of the former. There are those of us who serve for various reasons, most of them noble reasons (to pay it forward), that are not necessarily motivated by love. And, unfortunately, there are those of us who serve with ulterior motives.

As one commentator exhorted: "Serve, not for the good feelings you get from it. Serve, not because it looks good on a resume or college application. Serve, not because it looks good on Facebook, Twitter, or Instagram. Serve, for the benefit of others. Serve, because you want to model your life on the greatest person who ever lived. Serve, because Jesus was a servant. Serve, because you want to be like Him. Serve, because that is what it looks like to be truly great in this upside-down, radical, countercultural Kingdom that we call the Kingdom of God."[157]

There is no doubt that service motivated by Christlike, i.e., unconditional, love provides a unique blessing. For the servant, service provides an opportunity to express their love for others in tangible ways. For the recipient, service results in a no-strings-attached blessing. The life of our Lord and Savior reflects this dynamic. His life and death were tangible expressions of His love for us. Our salvation is a blessing that does not come with any strings attached.

It is not surprising then that one who reads the New Testament is likely to recognize how often loving and serving are connected. Galatians 5:13 is representative. *"Constantly love each other and be committed to serve one another."*

The essays in Part Four suggest ways we can serve collectively and individually. Their goal is to examine how service motivated by love can make a difference in our society.

Chapter 10: Transforming Society: How to Make Disciples of Nations recognizes that Jesus is a perfect role model for transforming society. With Jesus as our role model, we will be different, think differently, and act differently in pursuit of the goal to establish the culture of Heaven on the earth.

Chapter 11: The Social Transformation Framework: A Model for Launching Kingdom-Minded Movements sets forth the social transformation framework. It is a template, i.e., a repeatable process, for using a Kingdom-minded social impact movement to create transformation. The Framework identifies and defines essential components of such a movement.

Chapter 12: Apostolic Governance: Bringing Kingdom Culture Into Our Sphere of Influence is an essay that sheds new light on the term "apostle." It helps us understand we have a mandate to do what we can to establish Kingdom culture in our sphere of influence.

Chapter Ten

Transforming Society: How To Make Disciples Of Nations

I suppose we could discuss how to bring about social transformation without relying on the greatest social transformer of all time as a guide; but that would be like developing a discipleship program without quoting the Bible, singing a worship song without mentioning God, or attending a church service without talking to anyone.

We could do it. But it wouldn't mean much.

So, let's start our meaningful discussion of how to accomplish social transformation, i.e., how to disciple a nation, by focusing on the greatest social transformer of all time, Jesus of Nazareth.

It's quite an understatement to say that Jesus' ministry did more than tinker with the status quo. He wasn't interested in incremental changes ("love your enemies" qualifies as a sea change). Nor was He interested in placating the leaders of His day ("woe to you, scribes and Pharisees, hypocrites!" didn't exactly endear Him to the religious leaders). Nor was He interested in telling people what they wanted to hear ("go sell all you have and give it to the poor," which was not what the rich young ruler was expecting).

Jesus came to transform His world.

And what did His first-century world look like? It's worth examining some of the dynamics of Jesus' society to provide a context for Jesus as a social transformer. Such an examination will also help us understand that social transformation may sometimes be necessary, but it is not always welcomed.

Moreover, it is helpful to discuss twenty-first century transformation within the context of first-century transformation to understand that the principles of social transformation used by Jesus are applicable today.

When we look at the world around us, even the thought of transforming society can be daunting. As Anglican Priest and theologian John R. W. Stott said in his book *"The Message of the Sermon on the Mount"*:

> "[T]he very notion that Christians can exert a healthy influence in the world should bring us up with a start. What possible influence could the people described in the beatitudes exert in this hard, tough world? What lasting good can the poor and the meek do, the mourners and the merciful, and those who try to make peace not war? Would they not simply be overwhelmed by the floodtide of evil? What can they accomplish whose only passion is an appetite for righteousness, and whose only weapon is purity of heart? Are not such people too feeble

to achieve anything, especially if they are a small minority in the world?"[158]

But Stott reminds us that "Jesus did not share this skepticism. Rather the reverse. The world will undoubtedly persecute the church; yet it is the church's calling to serve this persecuting world."[159]

One of the first lessons to be learned from the greatest social transformer of all time is that transforming society is not just something we *should* do as His followers; it is something *we are called to* do.

LESSONS FROM JESUS THE GREAT SOCIAL TRANSFORMER

A Comparison of the First and Twenty-first Centuries

In the first-century, with such diverse groups as the Zealots, the Sadducees, the Pharisees, and the Essenes, religion and politics were intertwined in a rather complex way.[160] Jesus' unique ability to lay the foundation for transformation during such complexity provides the twenty-first century transformer with several lessons.

Like first-century Jerusalem, religion and politics in America are intertwined in a complex way. America is a complex mixture of social, political, and religious

---

158 R.W. Stott, *The Message of the Sermon on the Mount* (InterVarsity Press. Downers Grove, IL 1978), 57.

159 Stott, *The Message of the Sermon on the Mount, 57.*

160 Gerard Hall, "The World of Jesus' Time," *Jesus The Christ": A Christology Course,* accessed May 14, 2018 https://resource.acu.edu.au/gehall/XTOLOGY2.htm

ideologies. Its political mix includes, but is certainly not limited to, the "Progressive Left," which contains a humanistic worldview, and the "Religious Right," which includes a Christian worldview.

They are intertwined with a religious mix that includes, but is certainly not limited to, "Fundamentalists," whose focus includes the Word of God, and "Evangelicals," whose focus includes the supernatural power of God.

The similarities between social groups during Jesus' day and social groups in contemporary American society may be broad. However, there are some specific lessons we can learn from Jesus' interaction with these groups.

Among the lessons are, that like Jesus, social transformers must engage the broader segments of society. They cannot operate strictly or mainly "within the four walls" of the church. See, Jesus' choice of dining partners, i.e., tax collectors.

Social transformers must forge ahead even though others may see them as a radical threat to the established order. When they advocate for positions that are inconsistent with or in opposition to positions taken by certain well-established groups currently "in power," resistance is sure to arise. See, Matthew 21:12-13 (NKJV) "my house shall be called a house of prayer."

Social transformers must follow the leading of God's Word even when others accuse them of relativizing the scriptures. Such accusations sometimes fly when social transformers use the Word to support their efforts to address societal ills such as poverty as well as saving souls. See, Matthew 25:31-40.

Social transformers must resist the temptation to beat people at their own game. As Jesus demonstrated by calling attention to the present way of thinking ("You have heard that it was said to those of old . . . ") before advocating for a new way of thinking ("But I say to you . . . "), society cannot be transformed by using the same thinking that created the current society. See, Matthew 5:21-48 (NKJV).

In summary, despite all the obstacles and opposition, social transformers must be different from society to make society different from what it is now.

To bring about Social Transformation, We must be Different, We must Think Differently, and We must Act Differently

If we are to influence society, we must be active participants in society. However, as Stott noted in *The Message of the Sermon on the Mount*, "The influence of Christians in and on society depends on their being distinct [from the rest of society]."[161]

"There is a fundamental difference," he continues. "Between Christians and non-Christians, between the church and the world. ... This theme is basic to the Sermon on the Mount. The Sermon is built on the assumption that Christians *are* different, and it issues a call to us to *be* different."[162]

As Jesus said during The Sermon:

---

161 Stott, *The Message of the Sermon on the Mount, 60.*
162 Ibid, *63.*

"You have heard that it was said, 'You shall love your neighbor and hate your enemy.' But I say to you, love your enemies, bless those who curse you, do good to those who hate you, and pray for those who spitefully use you and persecute you, that you may be sons of your Father in heaven; for He makes His sun rise on the evil and on the good, and sends rain on the just and on the unjust. For if you love those who love you, what reward have you? Do not even the tax collectors do the same? And if you greet your brethren only, what do you do more than others? Do not even the tax collectors do so?" Matthew 5:43-48 (NKJV).

But not just different from society.

"Christians are to be different from both Pharisees and pagans, the religious and irreligious, the church and the world. That Christians are not to conform to the world is a familiar concept of the New Testament. It is not so well known that Jesus also saw (and foresaw) the worldliness of the church itself and called his followers not to conform to the nominal church either, but rather to be a truly Christian community distinct in its life and practice from the religious establishment, an *ecclessiola* (little church) *in ecclesia*. The essential difference in religion as in morality is that authentic Christian righteousness is not an external manifestation only, but one of the secret things of the heart."[163]

Thus, twenty-first century transformers are different from both a political spirit *and* a religious spirit. But they must

---

163 Ibid, 126

be careful as it relates to the latter. As Jesus said about the law, which some are eager to dismiss or diminish in favor of "a new and better covenant," "*I did not come to abolish the law but to fulfill it.*" See, Matthew 5:17 (NKJV).

Stott notes that some scholars look to the six "I say unto yous" (scholars know them as the six antitheses) in the Sermon on the Mount to support their position that Jesus "is inaugurating a new morality."[164] Not so, he says; Jesus was "explain[ing] the true meaning of the moral law with all its uncomfortable implications." In short, Jesus was not calling for the abolition of the law, nor was He calling for more obedience but rather a "deeper and deeper obedience."[165]

Similarly, the call for twenty-first century social transformers to be different is not about disconnecting from politics or religion. Rather, it is a call to go beyond political "positions" and religious "precepts" to engage in the deeper meaning of the inherent value of politics—a well-ordered society and religion—an intimate relationship with a good God.

This call does not require social transformers to step out of those realms. As Stott says, Jesus issues an "insistent call to His followers to be different" in "both spheres of righteousness."[166]

Be Different

Jesus provides two apt examples of how we are to be different.

---

164 Ibid, 76

165 Ibid, 75

166 Ibid, 125

Firstly, we are to be salt.

"You are the salt of the earth; but if the salt loses its flavor, how shall it be seasoned? It is then good for nothing but to be thrown out and trampled underfoot by men." Matthew 5:13 (NKJV).

As Dietrich Bonhoeffer emphasized, "Jesus does not say: 'You must be the salt.' It is not for the disciples to decide whether they will be salt of the earth, for they are so whether they like it or not, they have been made salt by the call they have received. ... The call of Christ makes those who respond to it the salt of the earth in their total existence."[167]

What does it mean to *be* salt?

"Christian saltiness is Christian character as depicted in the beatitudes, committed Christian discipleship exemplified in both deed and word," said Stott. "For effectiveness, the Christian must retain his Christlikeness, as salt must retain its saltness. If Christians become assimilated to non-Christians and contaminated by the impurities of the world, they lose their influence. ... Otherwise, if we Christians are indistinguishable from non-Christians, we are useless. We might as well be discarded like saltless salt, 'thrown out and trodden under foot by men.'"[168]

Secondly, we are to be light. *"You are the light of the world. A city that is set on a hill cannot be hidden. Nor do they light a lamp and put it under a basket, but on a lampstand, and it gives light to all who are in the house,"* Matthew 5:14-15 (NKJV).

---

167 Dietrich Bonhoeffer, *The Cost of Discipleship.* (Touchstone. NY, NY 1995), 116

168 Stott, *The Message of the Sermon on the Mount, 60.*

"Once again it is not: 'You are to be the light'; we are already the light because Christ has called us."[169] We are to let our light so shine before men that they will see our good works and glorify our Father. Matthew 5:16 (NKJV).

Good works have particular meaning for the social transformer for "The primary meaning of 'works' must be practical, visible deeds of compassion. It is when people see these, Jesus said, that they will glorify God, for they embody the good news of His love which we proclaim. Without them, our gospel loses its credibility and our God His honour."[170]

"A Christian's character as described in the beatitudes and a Christian's influence as defined in the salt and light metaphors are organically related to one another. Our influence depends on our character."[171]

What does this mean for the twenty-first century transformer?

According to Dick and Dr. Arleen Westerhof, it means a radical change in our thinking.

"God is restoring the truth that apostles, prophets, evangelists, pastors, and teachers are meant to equip believers for the works of service (Eph. 4:11-12)," they wrote in *New Perspectives on Apostolic Leadership*.[172]

---

169 Bonhoeffer, *The Cost of Discipleship*, 117

170 Stott, *The Message of the Sermon on the Mount*, 61

171 Ibid, 68

172 Bruce Cook, *Aligning with the Apostolic, Vol. 4: Apostles and Apostolic Movement In The Seven Mountains of Culture*. (Kingdom House Publishing. Lakebay, WA, 2012)

"No longer will it just be 'the anointed man or woman of God' who gets to minister. All of God's saints get to participate in God's Kingdom. This is going to require a radical change in how apostolic leaders think and act. Making this change, however, is imperative. If we do not, we will not see the Kingdom of God manifesting in and transforming our nations as God intended."[173]

As they imply, being different starts with understanding Ephesians 4:11-12—*And He Himself gave some to be apostles, some prophets, some evangelists, and some pastors and teachers, for the equipping of the saints for the work of ministry, for the edifying of the body of Christ*—differently (NKJV).

Both five-fold ministers ("Ministers") and the saints must view "ministry" differently. To minister literally means to serve. Both ministers and saints must expand their view of ministry. In many circles, the current view is that ministry happens on church grounds. It is initiated by the pastor. And it happens through church ministries. Ministers and saints must realize that serving can happen anywhere, any time, and with anyone.

When the definition of ministry is expanded to its full meaning, then ministers and saints will see themselves and each other differently.

The saint will stop relying on the minister to determine when and how they serve. They will recognize that their primary drive must be the God-given call and purpose in their lives. It is God, not the minister, who has prepared

---

173 Dick and Dr. Arleen Westerhof, "New Perspectives on Apostolic Leadership", *Aligning with the Apostolic, Vol. 4*, Kindle Edition, location 1220 & 1237.

good works for us in advance to do. The saints will realize ministers have been "given" to them as gifts by God to help them in their ministry.

When saints understand they play a critical role in advancing God's Kingdom, they will be more intentional about seeking the equipping necessary to achieve their calling and purpose effectively.

Ministers will no longer see their role as taking care of "their" sheep. They will understand their responsibility to equip God's saints for the saints' own unique work of ministry, i.e., serving.

Both the minister and the saint will realize that ministry makes the biggest difference when it results in "practical, visible deeds of compassion."[174] Such deeds not only demonstrate the love of God, but they also glorify God.

Think Differently

Jesus also asked His followers to think differently. For instance, a significant part of His Sermon on the Mount was spent demonstrating how to think differently about the law.

"Pharisees were content with an external and formal obedience, a rigid conformity to the letter of the law," said Stott. "Jesus teaches us that God's demands are far more radical than this. The righteousness which is pleasing to Him is an inward righteousness of mind and motive. For 'The Lord looks on the heart.'"

---

174 Stott, *The Message of the Sermon on the Mount,* 61

"It was a new heart-righteousness which the prophets foresaw as one of the blessings of the Messianic age. 'I will put my law within them, and I will write it upon their hearts,' God promised through Jeremiah (31:33)."[175]

This new "heart-righteousness" was demonstrated by Jesus when He was questioned about why He healed on the Sabbath. He did not explain His actions by denigrating the law of the Sabbath but by explaining its deeper meaning; the Sabbath was made for man, man was not made for the Sabbath. See, Mark 2:23-27 (NKJV).

Satisfying the search for deeper meaning as a part of thinking differently has particular relevance for the twenty-first century transformer.

Stott notes that there are "young people who feel frustrated in the modern world. The problems of the human community are so great, and they feel so small, so feeble, so ineffective."[176] He then asks,

"What message do we have, then, for such people who feel themselves strangled by 'the system', crushed by the machine of modern technology, overwhelmed by political, social and economic forces which control them and over which they have no control? They feel themselves victims of a situation they are powerless to change. What can they do?

"It is in the soil of this frustration," he responds. "That revolutionaries are being bred, dedicated to the violent overthrow of the system. It is from the very same soil

---

175 Ibid, 74
176 Ibid, 63

that revolutionaries of Jesus can arise, equally dedicated activists—even more so—but committed rather to spread His revolution of love, joy, and peace. And this peaceful revolution is more radical than any programme [sic] of violence, both because its standards are incorruptible and because it changes people as well structures."[177]

The Apostle Paul would say that thinking differently starts by renewing our minds: *"Do not be conformed to this world but be transformed by the renewing of your mind, that you may prove what is that good and acceptable and perfect will of God."* Romans 12:2 (NKJV).

The "revolutionaries of Jesus" conform to the world when trying to beat people at their own game. For instance, when they rely more on political processes than Kingdom values and Kingdom principles to change society.

To paraphrase Albert Einstein, you can't change a situation by using the same thinking that created it.

The "revolutionaries of Jesus" display a renewed mind when they are more committed to spreading His revolution of love, joy, and peace than electing the "right" candidates or advocating for laws that legislate more righteous behaviors.

When we renew our minds, when we have put off our old nature with its deeds and put on our new nature, which is renewed in knowledge according to the image of our Creator, i.e., when we think differently, we will display different behaviors. We will display Christlike love, "which is the bond of perfection." See, Colossians 3 (NKJV).

---

177 Ibid

Love is the foundation of a transformed culture but developing a transformed culture requires a new mindset, a transformation mindset. Because love is the foundation of a transformed culture, it is the principal element of a transformation mindset.

Below I have set forth the major elements of the Transformation Mindset. For illustration, I have compared it to a Church Mindset and a Kingdom Mindset.

I must give credit to Dr. Peter Wagner, who produced a much-relied-upon PowerPoint for Global Spheres Center that set forth the differences between churches and apostolic centers.[178] It is the primary source for what I have set forth below regarding the Church Mindset and the Kingdom Mindset. The basis of the Transformation Mindset was inspired by hearing Bob Hartley explain what God gave him regarding a Hope Mindset.[179]

Many times, when we see side-by-side comparisons, such as the one set forth below, there is a temptation to view one as better than the other. That is NOT the case here.

It takes intentionality to bring people to salvation and to disciple them. The Church Mindset brings that intentionality. It takes intentionality and a different mindset to equip saints for the work of ministry. The Kingdom Mindset brings that intentionality. Similarly, it takes intentionality and a different mindset to bring about the

---

178 C. Peter Wagner, *Apostolic Centers,* June, 2012, accessed https://gloryofzion.org/docs/Apostolic%20 Centers_sm.pdf

179 Bob Hartley and Michael Sullivant, M. "The Hope Reformation Room – An Angelic Encounter" *1Soul 1Nation.* October, 2012, accessed http://1soul1nation.blogspon.com/2012/10/bob-hartley-and-michael-sullivant-hope.html. ed. note: now flagged as a risky website by McAfee

transformation of society. The Transformation Mindset brings that intentionality.

Or, put another way, a Church Mindset is indispensable for saving souls, a Kingdom Mindset is indispensable for equipping saints for the work of ministry, and a Transformation Mindset is indispensable for replacing the current culture with a Kingdom Culture.

The three mindsets are not mutually exclusive, and they may operate simultaneously within the same sphere when necessary.

The Transformation Mindset: A Comparison of the Elements

Church Thinking	Kingdom Thinking	Transformation Thinking
	Overview	
Preach the Gospel	Light of the World	The Glory & Presence of God

An important goal of transformation is to increase the presence of God, His love, His grace, and His anointing to break yokes so that His supernatural power is displayed in real and tangible ways in society.

	Reliance on God	
The Word of God	The Power of God	The Power of Hope in God

People are motivated to be agents of transformation by a confident expectation of good from a good God. This hope in God compels them to take action.

The Principle Thing

Salvation	Equipping Saints	Called by Love /
[personal]	[for ministry]	Serve Others
		[to make His way known]

Everyone is a minister; they are motivated by Christlike love to serve others in their sphere of influence and to make God's ways known.

The Focus

Personal Renewal	Body of Christ	Cities & Nations

The focus of transformation is on all of society

Engaging People

Bring In	Send Out	Be Among
(to the church)	(to the world)	(the people/not of the people)

The transformation mindset recognizes that salt works best when it is mixed in, not poured on. There is no "them," just "us."

Retain Members	Release Saints	Help the Helpers

Partnerships/alliances are made with others who are transformers regardless of their affiliation so long as they display Kingdom values and are engaged in transformation

Leadership

Pastor-Led	Apostle-Led	Hope Fueled, Love-Led

Transformational acts are not just launched by leaders but motivated by hope and Christlike love; all types of people, regardless of role, engage in acts of service

Leadership Structure

| One Priest | Five-Fold Ministers | Every Person A Transformer |

Everyone in the community is a minister and is discipled, equipped, empowered, and encouraged to serve others regardless of their position or role [or lack thereof].

Leadership Activity

| Care for the Sheep | Mobilize the Army | Empower the People |

Everyone is empowered/encouraged to act in their sphere of influence to display Kingdom values and advance Kingdom principles.

Leadership Skills

| Three-Fold Gifts | Five-Fold Gifts | Knowledge, Skills, Abilities |

The effective display of skill and a consistent display of integrity give transformers the trust and credibility needed to exercise influence in their respective spheres of influence.

The Mindsets: A Summary

The Local Church: Establishing the People of God / Revival (souls are saved): We are Pastor-led, and we preach the Gospel. We rely on the Word of God to bring People to Church so they may experience Reconciliation with God and Personal Renewal. We retain People as Members so that our Priest can care for them and meet their needs. All of this is accomplished primarily by using the Three-Fold Gifts of evangelism, preaching, and teaching.

The Apostolic Center: Establishing the Kingdom of God / Reformation of the church (building the body of Christ): We are Apostle-Led. We are the Light of the World sent out into the world to perform signs, miracles, and wonders through the Power of God. We are equipped to perform the work of the ministry and to build the Body of Christ. The Five-Fold Ministers mobilize the Army and release the Saints to go forth and establish the Kingdom. All of this is accomplished using the Five-Fold Gifts.

The Transformation Mindset: Advancing the Kingdom of God / Transformation of society (Kingdom values and principles influence all of culture): We are Hope-fueled and Love-led. We are called by Love to serve others and in so doing, we bring the Glory and Presence of God into cities and nations. We are among the People and the Power of Hope in God motivates us to help people and to Help the Helpers as well. Every one of us is a transformer and we empower other people to bring about transformation in their sphere of influence. All of this is accomplished using our knowledge, skills, and abilities.

The Transformation Mindset is just one way of thinking differently. While thinking differently is a prerequisite to developing a transformed society, it is insufficient to create a transformed society. The twenty-first century transformer must also act differently.

Act Differently

Jesus asked His disciples to demonstrate that they were different by encouraging them to act differently. He modeled this for them (and for us) often.

For example, He asked His disciples to lead differently.:

> *"You know that the rulers of the Gentiles lord it over them, and those who are great exercise authority over them. Yet it shall not be so among you; but whoever desires to become great among you, let him be your servant. And whoever desires to be first among you, let him be your slave—just as the Son of Man did not come to be served, but to serve, and to give His life a ransom for many."* Matthew 20:25-28 (NKJV).

Then He demonstrated what servant leadership looks like in action.

> [He] *"rose from supper and laid aside His garments, took a towel and girded Himself. After that, He poured water into a basin and began to wash the disciples' feet, and to wipe them with the towel with which He was girded. ... So, when He had washed their feet, taken His garments, and sat down again, He said to them, 'Do you know what I have done to you? You call Me Teacher and Lord, and you say well, for so I am. If I then, your Lord and Teacher, have washed your feet, you also ought to wash one another's feet. For I have given you an example, that you should do as I have done to you.'"* John 13:4-15 (NKJV).

Displaying greatness through servant leadership rather than lording authority over others is one way for the twenty-first century transformer to act differently, but there is a change in behavior that could have an even greater impact on transforming society.

As Jack Graham of Prestonwood Baptist Church in Dallas, Texas, has said: "Revival will come when we get the walls down between the Church and *the community*" (emphasis added).[180]

We must focus on community, not just the marketplace, to transform society. A community has life 24/7, not just nine to five, seven days a week, not just Monday through Friday, in all locations we frequent, not just in the workplace. We are members of a community regardless of where we worship, where we work, or whether we work, and regardless of our occupation. "To be a disciple of Jesus means you are part of a community by definition."[181]

The Apostle Paul calls us to "corporate identity in his famous 'Body of Messiah' dissertation" in the twelfth chapter of 1 Corinthians.[182] We can glean from Paul's dissertation the attributes and the benefits of being part of a community.

We are many members of one community: *"For as the body is one and has many members, but all the members of that one body, being many, are one body, so also is Christ. For by one Spirit we were all baptized into one body—whether Jews or Greeks, whether slaves or free—and have all been made to drink into one Spirit. For in fact the body is not one member but many."* I Corinthians 12:12-14 (NKJV).

---

180 See, C. Peter Wagner, *Spiritual Warfare Strategy: Confronting Spiritual Powers.* (Destiny Image. Shippensburg, PA 2011), Kindle Edition

181 Doug Greenwold, "Two Very Different Worlds: Western Evangelicalism and the Gospels," *Preserving Bible Times,* accessed May 14, 2018 http://preservingbibletimes.org/wp-content/uploads/2014/03/Reflection.TwoWorlds1.pdf

182 P. Herring, "Living Truth – the Hebraic Mindset" *Circumcised Heart.* February, 2010, *accessed May 14, 2018* http://circumcisedheart.info/Christian%20site/Living%20Truth%20-%20the%20Hebraic%20Mindset.pdf

Each one of us has value: *"If the foot should say, 'Because I am not a hand, I am not of the body,' is it therefore not of the body? And if the ear should say, 'Because I am not an eye, I am not of the body,' is it therefore not of the body? If the whole body were an eye, where would be the hearing? If the whole were hearing, where would be the smelling? But now God has set the members, each one of them, in the body just as He pleased. And if they were all one member, where would the body be?"*
I Corinthians 12:15-19 (NKJV).

No matter who we are, the community needs us: *"But now indeed there are many members, yet one body. And the eye cannot say to the hand, 'I have no need of you'; nor again the head to the feet, 'I have no need of you.' No, much rather, those members of the body which seem to be weaker are necessary. And those members of the body which we think to be less honorable, on these we bestow greater honor; and our unpresentable parts have greater modesty, but our presentable parts have no need."*
I Corinthians 12:20-23 (NKJV).

What happens to one in the community happens to all:
"But God composed the body, having given greater honor to that part which lacks it, that there should be no schism in the body, but that the members should have the same care for one another. And if one member suffers, all the members suffer with it; or if one member is honored, all the members rejoice with it."
I Corinthians 12:24-26 (NKJV).

Through Christ, we are a community of one: *"Now you are the body of Christ, and members individually."*
I Corinthians 12:27 (NKJV).

God created human beings to be in a community. "Our true and most complete meaning is derived from and experienced through our relationships with God and with other human beings."[183] The community benefits when each member of the community does their part: "*But, speaking the truth in love, may grow up in all things into Him who is the head—Christ—from whom the whole body, joined and knit together by what every joint supplies, according to the effective working by which every part does its share, causes growth of the body for the edifying of itself in love.*" Ephesians 4:15-16 (NKJV).

Paul makes it clear in these passages that each member of the community benefits by being part of the community and that the community benefits from each member.

In 2 Corinthians 8, he sets forth an example of the benefits that accrue when the members of one community engage in collective action to benefit another community. This chapter details how the Macedonians financially assisted destitute Christians whom they did not personally know in Jerusalem.[184]

Engaging in collective action requires us to make an exchange. We must let go of our separate and solitary pursuits to change *our* world (the result of a Western mindset of rugged individualism). Instead, we must embrace collective actions that can change *the* world.

Such collective action is possible through a social impact movement. A social impact movement is defined as an organized set of constituents pursuing a common agenda

---

183 P. Herring, "Living Truth – the Hebraic Mindset"

184 See, IVP New Testament Commentary Series – Paul Sets Forth Guidelines And Models Of Christian Stewardship. *BibleGateway, accessed* https://www.biblegateway.com/resources/ivp-nt/Paul-Sets-Forth-Guidelines

of change through collective action. It plays a particularly important role in transformation.[185]

We will examine a framework for creating a social impact movement in the next chapter.

---

185 Jessica Horn, Gender and Social Movements: Overview Report, BRIDGE, UK: *Institute of Development Studies*, pg. 9, October, 2013, accessed https://opendocs.ids.ac.uk/opendocs/bitstream/handle/20.500.12413/10898/Gender%20and%20social%20movements%20overview%20report.pdf?sequence=1&isAllowed=y

Chapter Eleven

The Social Transformation Framework: A Model For Launching Kingdom-Minded Movements

The social impact movement is the principal component of a framework that God is revealing to me that we can use to advance sustainable transformation. This revelation began the night that Pastor Ché Ahn, the President of Harvest International Ministry ("HIM"), commissioned me as an apostle in August of 2016. That night Stacey Campbell prophesied that "God is granting you a prophetic and strategic template that can be used in many many countries and you are going to teach not just on an educational level but actually a template to disciple and reform nations."

Less than forty-eight hours later, Lisette Malmberg, an HIM apostle in Aruba, was in my living room inviting my wife and me to help her launch a social impact movement. We accepted the invite, sold our house and cars, and moved to Aruba.

Lisette successfully launched the HopeAruba Movement a few months later, and as of this writing, she has created a groundswell of support across the major spheres of Aruban society. She is both the catalyst and the beneficiary of the "prophetic and strategic template" that Stacey Campbell prophesied the Lord would give me. I call it the Social Transformation Framework.

THE SOCIAL TRANSFORMATION FRAMEWORK

The idea of social transformation is not new. We do not lack social transformers. However, no less an authority than Peter Wagner wrote in 2010, "We have been doing everything we know how to do to see our cities transformed. However, after twenty years, we cannot point to a single city in America that has been reformed according to objective sociological measurements."[186] With all the upheaval we have seen since 2010, I dare say this situation has not changed.

How, then, can we accomplish sustainable social transformation?

The foundation of sustainable social transformation is a social impact movement with guiding principles that enlist people as the instruments of change, not just the beneficiaries of change. These change agents are called by love to serve others in their community. They possess a Transformation Mindset (outlined in the previous chapter) and a love for their community. In addition, they:

---

186 Che Ahn, *The Reformers Pledge* (Destiny Image. Shippensburg, PA 2010), 196

- ❖ take accountability for the betterment of their community,

- ❖ are engaged in collective action to achieve that betterment, and

- ❖ know how to use the tools of transformation.

These are the people who take the actions which are at the heart of the framework.

Overview of the Framework

The social transformation framework ("Framework") is a template, i.e., a repeatable process, for using a social impact movement to create transformation. The Framework identifies and defines essential components of such a movement ("Movement"). It also describes how those components relate to one another.

THE FRAMEWORK

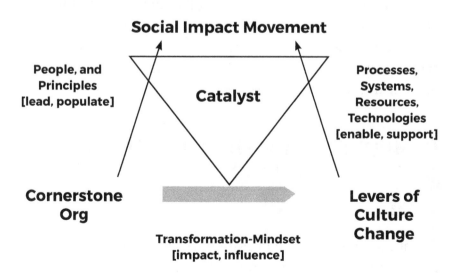

But the Framework does not contain step-by-step instructions on how to "build" transformation. Those steps should be dictated by each "agenda of change." Similarly, the Framework does not set forth the critical elements that support each of the components. For example, the Framework identifies "principles" as one of the components that "Cornerstone Organizations" supply to "The Movement." However, the Framework does not specify what those principles should be. Again, each specific agenda of change will dictate those elements.

Because it is a framework and not a "how-to" guide, it applies to a variety of movements. Among the possibilities are movements led by civic society organizations (non-political, non-religious) and movements led by religious bodies, e.g., church-led movements.

Given the nature of the social transformation we are discussing in this book, the following discussion of the Framework will focus on a Kingdom-led Movement. It is a movement that encourages collective action by followers of Christ and other people of goodwill who want to increase the display of Kingdom values, e.g., love and service, and Kingdom principles, e.g., the importance of responding to "the least of these."

COMPONENTS OF THE FRAMEWORK

The Movement

Social movements have been defined as forms of collective action that emerge in response to social inequality, oppression, or unmet social, political, economic, or cultural demands. They are comprised of an organized set of constituents pursuing a common agenda of change through collective action. The movement's catalyst initially articulates this agenda. A vision, mission, values, strategic framework, and guiding principles are developed as she engages other leaders.

As a tool for social transformation, the Movement is driven by a desire to see the increased presence of an agreed-upon set of values and principles, i.e., moral virtues that are the substance and meaning of life[187]

A Kingdom-led Movement is defined as a form of collective action motivated by a Christlike love to serve people. A key purpose of a Kingdom-led Movement is to see Kingdom values and Kingdom principles displayed in society to transform that society.

The social transformer must possess a Transformation Mindset that values collective action by a community to advance the movement.

A Kingdom-led Movement may be propelled by different ways of thinking. For example, its leaders may view the community as the foundation of the extended church rather than the marketplace. However, its goals are rooted in "right conduct" rather than "right thinking."[188]

Thus, a Kingdom-led Movement includes believers in Christ and what Dr. Peter Wagner describes as people

---

187 Brian Knowles, "The Hebrew Mind vs The Western Mind", *Thy Kingdom Came,* accessed https://thykingdomcame.com/the-hebrew-mind-vs-the-western-mind/

188 Ibid

of goodwill. There is no doctrinal litmus test. Such a movement is populated by people who are motivated by love to enable collective action that improve the spiritual, physical, emotional/mental, relational, and financial well-being of the members of their community.

A Kingdom-led Movement is launched by the God-given vision of an apostle. It is populated, in part, by followers of Christ who are salt and light. Thus, one of their primary motivations for the "good works" they perform is to glorify the Father. These good works also provide ample opportunity for ambassadors of Christ to carry out their ministry of reconciliation.

The Movement's Catalyst

The Catalyst is the Movement's visionary. She is instrumental in launching the Movement. She will typically be a leader who has the desire to transform her society. She will possess a vision for the future of her society. She either has or has access to the wherewithal, resources, and other means necessary to launch a social movement in pursuit of that vision. She will surround herself with an advisory council.

In a Kingdom-led Movement, the catalyst is normally someone who operates in the office of the apostle and is anointed with the accompanying gifts. She has received a vision from God, consistent with her mantle and metron, for the transformation of society. She engages others, including those in five-fold ministry offices, in the launch of the Movement.

The apostle becomes a catalyst for a social impact movement when she 1) makes plain the vision of transformation based on what she has heard from God and 2) gathers a group to provide counsel about launching and advancing the movement. Everything she does is rooted in a Kingdom perspective.

The apostle who leads a social impact movement is active and influential in society. She is a recognized leader in several spheres of culture. She leads an apostolic center (an apostle-led "entity" that is focused on making, equipping, and releasing disciples who embrace their identity, understand their assignment, and advance the Kingdom of God). She is also instrumental in bringing the "local" ekklesia into the Movement.

Because she understands that a spiritual battle accompanies social transformation efforts, she also enlists the help of an intercessory prayer team experienced in spiritual warfare. Intercession is a powerful weapon and it serves a vital purpose. This team should not be an after-thought or an add-on, but it should be considered an indispensable part of advancing the movement.[189]

Leadership by the apostle includes elements of the servant leadership model. One of her primary roles is to serve the people as they are equipped for the work of transformation. She does not treat the people who are participating in the Movement as servants of her vision. She does not ask the people what they can do for her. She asks the people what she (and the Movement) can do for them.

---

189 See, Tommi Femrite, *Invading The Seven Mountains With Intercession: How to Reclaim Society through Prayer* (Creation House. Lake Mary, FL 2011)

The Movement's Cornerstone

An organization or a group of organizations become a cornerstone of a social impact movement when 1) its leaders empower, equip, and release its people to become a significant part of the core group that launches, supports, and advances the Movement, 2) it supplies the Movement with values and guiding principles, and 3) it plays an instrumental role in using the levers of culture change to achieve the goals and objectives of societal transformation.

In a Kingdom-led Movement, this group of organizations is part of the Ekklesia. For purposes of a Kingdom-led Movement, the Ekklesia is defined as "that institution which assembles in His name, and which is composed of people who sustain a certain relationship to Him, i.e., people in Christ."[190] It consists of an assembly of "local" Christ-centered organizations that have come together to act as one body for the purposes of the Movement.

The leaders of the Ekklesia, including the Catalyst and her group of advisors, develop the values, principles, and transformation mindset that guide the Movement. They also provide the initial financial, technological, facility, and equipment resources that launch the Movement. They sustain the movement during its early stages.

An important role for the leaders of the Ekklesia is to supply the Movement with mature sons and daughters of God who become the core group of leaders and influencers.

---

190 See, Abiline Christian Word Study. The Cornerstone/Ekklesia is anchored by an apostolic center (or group of apostolic centers).

These "saints" and other people of goodwill who volunteer their time to Movement activities are critical to furthering the Movement's vision. Thus, the Ekklesia needs to help saints grasp the deeper meaning of Ephesian 4—they are ministers, and they must be equipped to fulfill their calling and purpose. Thus, their volunteer activities should be aligned with their God-given destiny.

These volunteers help the Movement by, among other things, serving in their areas of expertise, e.g., planning, logistics, accounting, and recruiting others to do the same.

In addition, the Ekklesia takes steps to instill a Transformation Mindset in the leaders who operate within the spheres of culture; thus, populating the marketplace with Kingdom-minded leaders who possess not only the maturity and the mindset but the credibility (competence and character) to affect their respective spheres of influence.

Examples of this influence include:

✤ using Kingdom principles to shape cultural values (arts & entertainment);

✤ infusing Kingdom principles into economic models, policies, and activities, e.g., relational economy, social entrepreneurship (business/economy);

✤ establishing values-based curriculum in schools (education);

✤ using Kingdom principles to establish environments in which healthy, whole, and stable extended families can thrive (family);

❖ establishing Kingdom-based good governance models that enable and support principle-based action by people, communities, and governments (government/ political);

❖ using Kingdom principles to produce vehicles of communication that are largely free of bias and resistant to manipulation (media); and

❖ creating a Kingdom-centered cultural atmosphere that supports spiritual growth (religion/spirituality).

Levers of Culture Change

A lever is a means of persuading or of achieving an end. Because the goals of a movement can vary, the type of lever used by movement leaders to achieve the movement's goals can vary. Depending on the type of movement and the nature of the transformation being pursued, the levers of culture change could be people, institutions, political activism, legislative agendas, demonstrations, etc. For example, non-violence was a lever of culture change used by the civil rights movement of the 1960s.

One of the primary goals of a Kingdom-led Movement is a society rooted and grounded in Kingdom values and Kingdom principles. The hallmarks of such a society are not just the absence of such things as hunger, thirst, and homelessness (Matthew 25) but the presence of prosperity ("Beloved, I pray that you may prosper in all things and be in health, just as your soul prospers." 3 John, NKJV). Because the heart, soul, mind, and strength of individuals matter (See, Mark 12:30), prosperity is not just financial prosperity but physical, mental/emotional, relational, and spiritual prosperity as well.

To achieve its goals, the levers of culture change in a Kingdom-led Movement must be designed to achieve prosperity in all respects. Thus, the Levers of Culture Change in a Kingdom-led Movement are designed to influence the major spheres of cultural influence. An individual sphere of influence shapes the way people think about that particular area of culture. These major spheres are—arts & entertainment (including sports), business/economics, education, family, government/politics, media, and religion.

The Levers of Culture Change enable the Movement by supplying it with processes, systems, technologies, resources, and ways of working that facilitate the accomplishment of the Movement's key purpose—to see the glory of God and His kingdom principles displayed in society in a way that transforms that society.

Kingdom-led leaders advance transformation within their respective spheres by, for example, using Kingdom principles to:

- shape cultural values (arts & entertainment/increase relational well-being);
- infuse Kingdom values into economic models, e.g., relational economy, social entrepreneurship (business/ increase financial well-being);
- establish values-based curriculum in schools (education/increase relational well-being); and
- establish environments where healthy, whole, and stable extended families can thrive (family/shape physical well-being).

THE FRAMEWORK IN ACTION

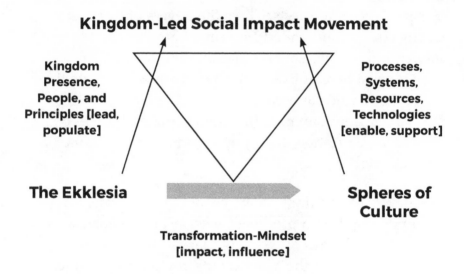

Kingdom-Led Social Impact Movement

Kingdom
Presence,
People, and
Principles [lead,
populate]

Processes,
Systems,
Resources,
Technologies
[enable, support]

The Ekklesia

**Spheres of
Culture**

**Transformation-Mindset
[impact, influence]**

THE SUSTAINABILITY OF
TRANSFORMATION

A movement that is initiated, launched and supported in
a genuinely apostolic and transformational way eventually
outgrows the reach of the Catalyst who started it. A servant
leader does not ask people to relinquish their vision to
support her vision; instead, she asks people to align their
vision, if possible, with the vision of the Movement.

Thus, a successful social impact movement is eventually
led by many servant leaders who share a common mindset
as well as Kingdom values and Kingdom principles. This
dynamic contributes to the sustainability of transformation
because transformation does not rise or fall with one leader
or even one set of leaders.

Some of the enemies of sustainability include:

* the termination of a "hot button" issue that galvanized initial support (either through successful resolution or a catastrophic setback);
* changes in the social, economic, or political landscape, e.g., an economic downturn or the loss of a key ally; or
* fatigue on the part of the leaders or the participants.

The existence of the Framework can mitigate these dangers. The Movement is values-driven, not outcome-driven; thus, the absence of a hot button issue is not fatal. When the goal is to establish and live according to a set of agreed-upon values rather than achieve a specific outcome, the Movement is less impacted by social upheaval, economic downturns, or a toxic political atmosphere.

Moreover, some social transformation efforts either fail outright or grow and then whither because the leaders did not establish the most important element of a strong foundation, a committed group of people. Even though time is precious, leaders must take the time to:

* gain buy-in from key leaders and other influential people of the vision, to the mission, values, and guiding principles of the Movement;
* gain buy-in for the development and the expected outcomes of transformation initiatives;
* achieve consensus on how to achieve transformation,
* instill within the people a Transformation Mindset as well as the Movement's values and principles (they

must be role models for that which they are bringing to pass), and

✤ equip the equippers and train the trainers.

Another way to increase the chances of sustainable social transformation is to use a consensus-driven process to develop (and then adhere to) guiding principles that focus not only on sustainability but also on accountability, responsibility, creativity, unity, and legacy.

These guiding principles, along with a group of committed people, will significantly increase the chances of a sustainable transformation.

FINAL THOUGHT: LOVE

We have learned from the greatest social transformer of all time that to make a difference in society, we must be different from the society we are trying to transform. We must think differently than the thinking we used to create the current state of affairs. We must act differently than our Western mindset has taught us.

However, the greatest lesson to be learned from the greatest social transformer of all time flows from the greatest commandments to display unconditional love.

Love is the foundation of transformation. Episcopalian Bishop The Most Reverend Michael Curry quoted Charles Marsh in *The Beloved Community* to observe "Jesus began the most revolutionary movement in human history: a movement grounded in the unconditional love of God for the world and a movement mandating people to live that love, and in so doing to change not only their lives but the very life of the world itself.[191]

The twenty-first century social transformer cannot accomplish her mission without unconditional love. That's our final and most important lesson from Jesus.

As Bishop Curry said about Him: "He gave up His life, He sacrificed His life, for the good of others, for the good of the other, for the well-being of the world... for us. That's what love is. Love is not selfish and self-centered. Love can be sacrificial, and in so doing, becomes redemptive. And that way of unselfish, sacrificial, redemptive love changes lives, and it can change this world."[192]

If we can love as Jesus loves, then perhaps we can be as transformative as He is.

Chapter Twelve

Apostolic Governance: Bringing Kingdom Culture Into Our Sphere Of Influence

In 2019, I wrote *Apostolic Governance in the 21st Century*. The primary focus of the book was to describe the activities involved in managing the behind-the-scenes activity of an apostolic center. I chose the term "governance" because it was a broader and more appropriate term than "management."

As I continue to study, meditate, and hear from the Lord on the topic of apostolic governance, I realize that the term has a broader application. We can understand this application by taking a separate look at the words that make up the term "apostolic governance."

APOSTOLIC

Luke 6:13 says, "And when it was day, He [Jesus] called His disciples to Himself; and from them He chose twelve whom He also named apostles."

Why did Jesus name the twelve "apostles"? A little background will help us understand the significance of the word and why it has meaning for us today.

As noted by Pastor Che Ahn in his book, *Modern Day Apostles:*[193]

> *"The word, "apostolos," is Greek. It means "sent out one."*[194] *The Greeks used the word to describe an admiral over a fleet of ships sent out by his king to conquer other territories and to establish his government in those territories."*[195]

> *"The Roman Empire that occupied Palestine during the time of Jesus also believed in this approach. As Rome conquered land and expanded its territory, the leaders of the Empire realized something important to their survival; unless they brought Roman culture to that conquered territory, the inhabitants of the land would revert to their previous culture and they would rebel against the Empire."* [196]

Simply put, an apostle, among other things, is one sent to a land to establish their culture in that land.

---

193 Che Ahn, *Modern Day Apostles: Operating In Your Apostolic Office And Anointing* (Destiny Image. Shippensburg, PA 2019)

194 Thayer, Joseph Henry. Greek-English Lexicon of the New Testament. New York: American (Harper), 1889. Blue Letter Bible. 1996-2012. 11 Jun. 2018 <http://www.blueletterbible.org/lang/lexicon/lexicon.cfm>.

195 Dr. Ron Cottle and Dr. John P. Kelly, "Apostles What Are They?," *International Coalition of Apostolic Leaders*, 2015, accessed https://www.icaleaders.com/about-ical/definition-of-apostle/

196 This concept was called Romanization. For a general discussion of Romanization see Marianne Sawicki, *Crossing Galilee: Architectures in the Occupied Land of Jesus* (Harrisburg, PA: Trinity Press International, 2000); see also Dr. Neil Faulkner, "Romanisation: The Process of Becoming Roman," *BBC*, February 17, 2011, accessed http://www.bbc.co.uk/history/ancient/romans/romanisation_article_01.shtml

To be apostolic is to be engaged in the act of establishing one's culture.

GOVERNANCE

Businessdictionary.com describes governance as: "The mechanisms, relations, and processes by which a corporation is controlled and is directed; [it] involves balancing the many interests of the stakeholders of a corporation."

This definition is framed by and limited by a particular environment, the corporate environment. But what if we freed the definition of governance from this limitation?

"Governance" could be defined as "the mechanisms, relations, and processes by which a home [classroom, office space, gym, movie set, theater, homeless shelter, social media forum, ministry, or corporation] is controlled and is directed; it involves balancing the many interests of the stakeholders of a home [classroom, office space, gym, movie set, theater, homeless shelter, social media forum, ministry, or corporation]."

To govern is to control or direct an enterprise (ministry or business), a group of people (family or team), or an environment (home, workplace) through the use of "mechanisms, relations, and processes."

APOSTOLIC GOVERNANCE IS A KINGDOM ASSIGNMENT

Understanding these two words helps us to realize that apostolic governance is a Kingdom assignment.

Not all of us have been called by God to the office of apostle, but each of us can be apostolic.

To be apostolic is to be engaged in the act of establishing a different culture. To govern is to control or direct an enterprise or a group of people or an environment through the use of "mechanisms, relations, and processes."

Thus, apostolic governance means to be engaged in the act of bringing culture from our "home" territory to an enterprise, group of people, or an environment we control or direct through the use of "mechanisms, relations, and processes."

As disciples of Jesus, apostolic governance means bringing Kingdom culture into our sphere of influence through the use of mechanisms (acts of service motivated by Christlike love), relations (loving unconditionally, displaying God's grace, mercy, and forgiveness), and processes (prayer, intercession, and spiritual warfare).

Cutting through all of my analogies, each of us can increase the presence of Kingdom principles and values in our respective spheres of influence by acts of service motivated by Christlike love, displaying God's goodness, and praying.

The good news is that we don't have to be ordained ministers. We don't need Bible school training. We don't need to be part of an organized ministry.

By understanding apostolic governance, parents, teachers, athletes, performers, students, business people, politicians, deacons, journalists, etc., can embrace our ability and assignment to help establish Kingdom culture on the earth.

Part Five:

Being Made Perfect In Love, Rethinking Ministry To Incorporate A New Model Of Service

In Part One, we highlighted the importance of Christlike love. We become great by learning how to love unconditionally.

In Part Two, we discussed loving our neighbors as ourselves. We become great by being true neighbors, that is, expressing our love through serving others.

In Part Three, we examined loving people with whom we have differences. We become great by loving those who may regard us as enemies.

In Part Four, we recognized that we cannot love without serving. We become great by serving others motivated by Christlike love.

In this part, we examine the Apostle Paul's statement in Ephesians 4:16. "Every member has been given divine gifts to contribute to the growth of all." We become great by equipping, empowering, and encouraging each member of the Body of Christ to serve in their sphere of influence.

The essays in Part Five ask us to think differently about how we approach ministry and who gets to minister. The goal is to suggest ways to unleash even more people into service that benefits our society.

Chapter 13: All of God's Saints Get to Minister: A Radical Change in How Apostolic Leaders Think and Act takes a deeper look at Chapter 4 of Ephesians. It advocates for changes in how we view the role of the five-fold minister and the saint they are equipping.

Chapter 14: Practicing What We Preach: Equipping the Saints in Ministry Work Environments is part two of the discussion of Ephesians 4. Chapter 13 discussed how ministers could equip saints in the pews for the work of ministry. This essay suggests that incorporating family values in ministry workplaces is one way that ministers can equip saints who work for ministries for the work of ministry.

Chapter Thirteen

All Of God's Saints Get To Minister: A Radical Change In How Apostolic Leaders Think And Act

According to Dick and Dr. Arleen Westerhof: "No longer will it just be 'the anointed man or woman of God' who gets to minister," they say. "All of God's saints get to participate in God's Kingdom. This is going to require a radical change in how apostolic leaders think and act. Making this change, however, is imperative. If we do not, we will not see the Kingdom of God manifesting in and transforming our nations as God intended."[197]

Let's explore those radical changes.

As the Westerhofs imply, our radical change in thinking begins with understanding Ephesians 4:11-12 (NKJV)—*And He Himself gave some to be apostles, some prophets, some evangelists, and some pastors and teachers*[198]*, for the equipping of the saints for the work of ministry, for the edifying of the body of Christ*—differently.

RADICAL CHANGE #1:
HOW WE VIEW MINISTRY

Both five-fold ministers ("Ministers") and the Saint must view "ministry" differently. To minister means to serve. Thus, ministry does not just occur on church grounds, during church services, or with church people. Ministry can happen anywhere, any time, and with anyone.

Thus, ministry can be operating a performing arts academy or coaching a soccer team as well as discipling a youth group. It can be leading a professional association as well as leading a Bible study. When our activities serve others and advance Kingdom principles and values, we are engaged in ministry.

Ministry can take place anywhere. It can take place:

❖ at school as well as at church,

❖ in the break room as well as at the altar, and

❖ on the softball field as well as in the sanctuary.

To make such ministry a reality, we must expand our perception that pastors or elders initiate ministry. We must realize that we are all ministers (i.e., servants), and thus, anyone can initiate ministry. Jesus gave the five-fold gifts to equip the saints for this purpose.

RADICAL CHANGE #2:
HOW WE VIEW THE RELATIONSHIP
BETWEEN MINISTERS AND SAINTS

Statistics tell us that most churches in America are attended by less than 100 people.[199] Thus, many of us grow up with the image of the pastor being the jack of all trades, or at the least, in charge of everything.

The pastor preached the sermons on Sunday. He taught the midweek Bible studies. He approved the activities of the Evangelism Team, the Children's Church, and everything in between.

As a result, most church members were bystanders. To the extent members were involved in ministry, they were basically the pastor's assistants. Even in larger churches, the pastor-is-in-charge model prevailed.

Thus, church members (or to use the Ephesians 4:11 term "saints") relied on the pastor (or "minister") to equip them for the work of the local church. This meant that the saints were at the mercy of the minister in terms of how they were equipped.

We must view saints differently. We must recognize saints:

✤ are expected to walk worthy of the calling to which we have been called. Ephesians 4:1

✤ have been saved to do good works which God has prepared for us. Ephesians 2:8-10

---

199 Aaron Earls, "The Church Growth Gap: The Big Get Bigger While the Small Get Smaller," *Christianity Today,* March 6, 2019, accessed https://www.christianitytoday.com/news/2019/march/lifeway-research-church-growth-attendance-size.html

✤ are blessed by God with gifts He expects us to use.
   Romans 12:3
✤ have been given the ministry of reconciliation.
   2 Corinthians 5:17-20

Among the important implications of how saints are
viewed is how saints view themselves. The saints are
no longer just church members sitting in the pews on
Sundays and Wednesdays. They are not just ministry
assistants helping to run church ministries. They are
no longer just "consumers" of whatever equipping the
minister offers them.

To use an analogy, saints are like restaurant patrons. They
make a selection based on the menu developed by the chef.
For the saint, it is a take-it-or-leave-it proposition.

This situation must change.

Saints must understand that they play a critical role in
advancing God's Kingdom. Thus, they must become fully
engaged ministers who seek the equipping necessary to be
effective in achieving their calling and purpose.

The saint must stop relying on the minister to be the sole
determiner of when and how they serve. Our primary
driver must be the God-given call and purpose in our lives.
Ministers have been given to the saints as gifts by God to
help the saints in this pursuit.

From the saint's perspective, "God created me to perform
the good works He has prepared in advance for me to do.
He saved me for a purpose. The five-fold ministry gifts
exist to equip me for that purpose."

The script is flipped. The minister no longer equips the saint based on what the minister needs to operate the church's ministry. The minister equips the saint based on what the saint needs to perform the work of ministry that God has given him to do.

To use an analogy, saints are like gym patrons. The saint tells the personal trainer what she wants to accomplish in her workouts.

Yes, the personal trainer is the expert, but he does not have the latitude to develop a workout plan that the athlete is required to accept. The athlete decides whether she wants to gain strength, lose weight, or become more flexible. The personal trainer then equips the athlete based on this choice.

For this model to work, the minister must stop asking the saint what the saint can do for the ministry. The minister should start asking the saint what the minister can do for the saint (in terms of equipping them for the work of ministry).

Moreover, ministers must transition from just taking care of "their" sheep to also equipping God's ministers for their own unique work of ministry, i.e., serving.

As both the minister and the saint incorporate these radical changes in their thinking, they must continue to realize that ministry makes the biggest difference when it results in "practical, visible deeds of compassion."[200] Such deeds display the love of God, and they are what cause people to glorify God.

---

200 R.W. Stott, *The Message of the Sermon on the Mount* (InterVarsity Press. Downers Grove, IL 1995), 61

Chapter Fourteen

Practicing What We Preach: Equipping The Saints In Ministry Work Environments

Chapter Thirteen discussed the radical change in thinking that allowed "saints" in the church to move beyond the boundaries created by the traditional view of ministry. This change in thinking produces saints who are equipped to perform the good works God has prepared for them to do.

In this chapter, we will discuss the radical change in thinking that will allow ministries to equip their volunteers and their employees for the work of ministry.

Churches, and other ministry workplaces (hereinafter collectively referred to as "ministry"), are part of God's plan in this season to bring revival and reformation to Jerusalem, Judea, Samaria, and the uttermost parts of the earth. Unfortunately, a ministry's work environment is too often treated as if it is not located in any of those regions. By that, I mean ministry leaders are sometimes so focused on bringing revival and reformation to society that they do not focus on bringing revival and reformation to their own work environment.

In the movie, *Crimson Tide*, a submarine captain said: "We're here to preserve democracy, not to practice it."[201] The attitude of some ministry leaders appears to be: "We're here to advance Kingdom values, not to practice them."

This attitude does not prevail very often, but it is too often the case.

I don't pretend to be unaware of the reasons for the disconnect between what is preached in the pulpit and practiced in the ministry work environment. A work environment is a place of business, and we must treat it as such—"or else."

Or else there could be investigations of misconduct, or else there could be lawsuits filed, or else there could be fines levied. Of course, there is nothing wrong with avoiding these things. No one wants investigations, lawsuits, or fines.

But we can reduce the possibility of these things happening if we bring a Kingdom Mindset to work ("God's will be done at work as it is in heaven"). I am not saying that the ministry workplace should not be a place of business. I am saying we should bring business into a spiritual work environment rather than bringing the spiritual into a business environment.

One way to make this happen is to view the ministry as a family rather than an organization. As Bill Johnson

---

201 Crimson Tide Quotes, *IMDb*, accessed September 19, 2018 https://www.imdb.com/title/tt0112740/quotes

said, "Kingdom exists in family, not in organizations."
One might think ministry environments, given that their
inhabitants are followers of Jesus, already display the
attributes of family. Sadly, that is often not the case.

In my experience, the management of a ministry is similar
to the management of a corporation. The focus is on the
organization—meeting its goals, managing its people
and resources, and ensuring compliance with laws and
regulations.

Perhaps nothing represents this management mindset
more than the proliferation of human resources handbooks
in ministries. These handbooks are often developed by
lawyers or human resources professionals. Ministries adopt
them and follow them to protect themselves from potential
liability issues. They help ensure the ministry's compliance
with laws regarding harassment, discrimination, benefits,
confidentiality, etc.

Ministry leaders, who are accountable to the board of
directors for protecting the ministry's assets and shielding
the ministry from scandal, embrace a focus on compliance
in their work environment.

As stated earlier, there is nothing wrong with complying with
laws and regulations. No one wants investigations, lawsuits,
or fines. In other words, there are some valid reasons for
managing a ministry like an organization rather than a family.

But concepts such as obedience, following the rules,
avoiding trouble, i.e., compliance, are well known in
families. Operating a ministry with family values provides
additional benefits without substantial risks.

And the benefits are great.

A family relates to its members based on who they are; an organization relates to employees based on what they do.

A family member never loses her standing regardless of her behavior; an employee in an organization can lose her position based on her behavior (and she behaves accordingly).

A family member is motivated to help others do their best even at the expense of her best interests; an employee is motivated/incentivized to seek her best interests even at the group's expense.

The value of a family member is inherent; an employee must earn her value.

Families support one another in the pursuit of individual dreams; organizations require individuals to pursue only their goals.[202]

The leaders of a family prioritize the success of other family members. The leaders of an organization prioritize the success of the organization.

Families mature members to become independent; organizations require their employees to be compliant.

In families, obedience results from love; in organizations, obedience results from fear of consequences.

---

202 An individual's vision for his life need not be the same as the vision of the ministry but they do need to be aligned. This allows the individual to pursue his vision with all his heart, soul, mind, and strength while doing the same for the ministry's vision. It also allows the ministry to do the same.

Families are rooted and grounded in love; organizations are rooted and grounded in bylaws and handbooks.

As we know, a group rooted and grounded in love is more likely to serve others.

Of course, the members of a ministry family still have responsibilities for which they are compensated. Ministry is not just a family; everyone has a role. Yet, a ministry is about more than carrying out assigned responsibilities. The dynamics of a family color almost all actions and interactions. Thus, a family business is an appropriate analogy for the management side of a ministry.

No ministry is alike. Each ministry pursues its unique God-given calling. But every ministry shares a common goal—to grow the family business. As the Apostle Paul noted, Jesus has given each of us the ministry of reconciliation.

In a family business, the head of the family ensures that an individual's role is aligned with the goals of the business. This alignment allows each son and daughter in the family business to pursue their individual destiny in ways that also further the family business. The success of the individual member of the family and the success of the family business are both important. So, for example, a family member who loves relating to people and wants to pursue a career in a people-oriented profession would be given a role in interacting with people.

A ministry with a family DNA instead of an organizational DNA is more likely to equip family members for the work of ministry, i.e., the good works which the Lord has prepared in advance for them to do. To restate earlier comments in a more relevant and direct way, ministries that are managed like an organization:

- ❖ require individuals to pursue only its goals;
- ❖ prioritize the success of the organization; and
- ❖ require its employees to be compliant.

Of course, there's nothing wrong with any of these things. The point is not to criticize these things but to suggest a way to gain these benefits while also equipping saints for the work of ministry.

As noted earlier:

- ❖ families support one another in the pursuit of individual dreams;
- ❖ leaders of a family prioritize the success of other family members; and
- ❖ family members mature members to become independent.

Succinctly stated, ministries that operate more like families than organizations can pursue the ministry's God-given purpose while also providing its individual employees with an opportunity to perform the good works (serve) that God has prepared in advance for them to do.

It is another way for ministers to equip the saints for the work of ministry. It is another way to become great. It is another way to answer God's call to serve others.

Conclusion

We serve a God of paradoxes. He is the creator of the universe. Yet, He knows how many hairs are on our heads. He is all and in all. Yet, in Him, we live and move and have our being. He owns a thousand cattle on a thousand hills. Yet, the Son of Man had no place to lay His head.

God's Kingdom is a Kingdom of paradoxes. "It's an upside-down kingdom where leaders are servants, neighbors and enemies are loved, and poor widows give away half their money."[203]

Perhaps the most perplexing paradox is leaders as servants. Yet, we must master this paradox if America is going to become truly great. Not greatness on the global stage as in American exceptionalism, the Leader of the Free World, great. Greatness as defined by our Lord and Savior. To become great, we must serve motivated by Christlike love. Veritas Church in Lancaster, Pennsylvania expressed it well: "Serve, because that is what it looks like to be truly great in this upside-down, radical, countercultural Kingdom that we call the Kingdom of God."[204]

---

203 Preston Sprinkle, "Jesus' Upside Down Kingdom," *The Dietrich Bonhoeffer Institute, accessed* https://tdbi.org/devotionals/jesus-upside-kingdom/

204 "A Third Way To Follow Jesus, Week 11: Servanthood," *Veritas*, June 21, 2016, accessed https://veritas.community/veritas-community/athirdwayweek11

Each of us must become great by answering God's call
to serve others. To those of us willing to answer this call,
I pray the words of Jesus over us:

> *Lord, help us to lead by a completely different model; help
> us to live as ones who are called to serve others; give us
> the heart of a servant.*
>
> *Make each one of us great, Jesus; make America great.*
>
> *In your name, we pray. Amen*